PUBLISHING
& associates

Catch the Spirit of Prayer

Catch the Spirit of Prayer

Supernaturally Pray Out God's Plan for Your Life

Bruce Black
with Cindy Black

bush
PUBLISHING
& associates

COPYRIGHT

Unless otherwise indicated, all Scripture quotations are taken from the *New King James Version* of the Bible, copyright © 1979, 1980, 1982, Thomas Nelson, Inc., Publishers.
All Scripture quotations marked KJV are taken from the *King James Version* of the Bible.

Catch the Spirit of Prayer
Supernaturally Pray Out God's Plan for Your Life

ISBN Paperback: 978-1-944566-55-5
ISBN eBook: 978-1-944566-56-2
Copyright © 2024 Bruce Black & Cindy Black

Bush Publishing & Associates, LLC books may be ordered at everywhere and at Amazon.com
For further information, please contact:
Bush Publishing & Associates
Tulsa, Oklahoma
www.bushpublishing.com

Printed in the United States of America.

Table of Contents

Foreword

It was my joy and honor to share almost 40 years of my life and ministry with the man who held my heart and my hand.

Bruce was an amazing Bible teacher and a treasured gift to all of those he touched. His example of a life well lived in prayer and the Word is found in the pages of this book. He was a man of faith and love. He cherished the move of the Holy Spirit and he was undoubtedly a man of prayer!

Catch the Spirit of Prayer will encourage you, teach you, and empower you to follow the plan of God for your life fully. I believe it will inspire you to find your purpose and call as you pray in the Holy Spirit. Bruce gives real-life examples and teaches you how to implement the Word of God in prayer.

It is my heartfelt prayer that you *Catch the Spirit of Prayer* as you read this book.

Be Blessed,

Cindy Black

Introduction

"For I know the plans I have for you, declares the Lord, plans to prosper you and not to harm you, plans to give you hope and a future. Call upon Me, and you will come and pray to Me, and I will listen to you. You will seek Me and find Me when you seek Me with all your heart."

Jeremiah 29:11-13 NIV

Do you know you can supernaturally pray out God's plan and will for your life? God has a plan to prosper you and to give you hope. He has a wonderful future for you. How do you find God's will and the plan God has for *your* life? The Lord told Jeremiah to "come and pray" and "seek Him with all of his heart." The answers can be found in prayer! God's plans for your life will unfold to you as you pray.

Don't let another year go by where you just follow the course of this world. Don't make decisions based only on what you can see or by what you know in the "natural world" alone. You can learn to tap into the spirit realm. You can learn how to hear God's voice. You can go to the next level in your walk with the Lord by supernaturally praying for His plan and will in your life. It is a supernatural life that is filled with exciting days and it is available for *YOU!* Praise God!

The Way

by Cindy Black

I don't know if there is room for me;
I don't know exactly where to go…
I don't want to miss God's best,
or miss His supernatural flow.

I myself don't know the plan that my Father sees for me…
In the natural realm, there are details I simply can't see…
Oh, how can this be?

My mind, it tries to figure out
and show me every possible way…
It seems like I'm trying really hard to see my future here today!

This plan must first be prayed, and not just plotted out…
It's praying in the Holy Ghost by faith that brings it all about.

It is praying out a mystery…
Yes, it is a mystery to me…
but not to the Holy Ghost
who hears and knows the plan of God
that I cannot see!

How do I navigate? Who will I marry? Where exactly do I go?
My mind seems to want to explore every avenue,
and it still just does not know…

I look to the Greater One on the inside
who, in me, always does abide…
I look to him and His unchanging Word,
for that is the shadow of His wings and where I must hide!

I'm safe abiding in His love
and secure in His strong hand…
I trust Him who knows the road that I must walk,
because He leads me in His plan…

I trust the Lord, so in the Holy Ghost,
I begin to yield myself to pray...
I pray out the plan of God in other tongues, they are mysteries
that I say…

Not mysteries to the Lord of Lords
who knows every single thing,
but a mystery to my little brain
that tries to figure out, "What does this mean?"

I yield my tongue to the Spirit's ways, and mysteries through me
He does pray!
Intercession He makes on my behalf
in a heavenly, precious language:
I pray out my path...

From my belly flow rivers of living water…
From my belly, I begin to speak supernaturally to my father;
I pray out divine mysteries!

I will never be lost,
nor will I ever be disappointed
or dismayed.
When I pray His perfect will in the Holy Ghost,
He takes hold together with me today!

His spirit that lives greater in me
leads me into all truth,
until I can clearly see the plan of God
and clearly see my next move.

Oh, what a plan...
No fear... No sorrow...
No lack and No defeat...
When I pray in the mighty Holy Ghost,
He makes *The Way* for me!

Chapter One
A New Kind of Drunk

My story is not one of dramatic deliverance from drugs or destitution, nor alcohol or abominations. My wife, Cindy, says I grew up in a "Leave-It-To-Beaver" type of family. My mother and father were the "perfect" parents and I had the "perfect" middle-class childhood with plenty of love and support. However, even while I was growing up with all of this, I still had no idea of the amazing adventures God had planned for my life.

I graduated from high school in 1977 and was looking forward to enrolling in college that fall. All that I had ever wanted to do my whole life was be a professional trumpet player. My father was a band director and also a trumpet player. That helped open doors for me to play professionally at a very young age. I *loved* to play the trumpet! It just seemed natural for me to follow that course for my life, but God had other things in store for me.

More Than Just Trumpet Playing

In the fall of 1978, I started college. About that time, my father met this very interesting and sort of "strange" man from our mainline denominational church. I call him "strange" because he was different from everyone else in our church.

He wore this constant, funny smile on his face, and it seemed like he was always happy. It appeared that God blessed everything this man touched. He ran an international business from our small town in Illinois and drove a brand-new Mercedes Benz. Being 18 years old, those things naturally got my attention, but there was something else about him that was different. There was a presence about him. He walked in joy and peace no matter what was going on around him. He had a love for life and for other people that I had never seen or experienced before.

This man and my father became very good friends. They began to go places together. I wasn't really sure where they were going or what they were doing there, but I could see changes taking place in my father's life.

One weekend, I came home from college and noticed that the same great big smile that this man always wore was now on my father's face. It amazed me how different my father had become! He had always been such a good man, but now something had really altered his life as well. I curiously watched from a distance over the next few weeks as a marvelous change took place in our household.

A short time later I came home from school to find this little old man sitting in our living room again. He and my father had been talking for a while, so I snuck around the corner and sat down on the couch to listen to what they were saying.

They were telling some of the most amazing stories about what God had miraculously done. They were talking about how bodies had been healed and how miracles of divine protection had taken place. They shared testimonies about supernatural guidance in business and how God was abundantly prospering them. They kept mentioning this thing called "the baptism of the Holy Spirit." I'm sure they both knew God was setting me up to have a Holy Ghost encounter with Him.

Before I went back to college that weekend, my father gave me a book by a man I had never heard of before. His name was Rev. Kenneth E. Hagin. My father explained that if I had any questions about what had happened to him, Rev. Hagin's book and my Bible would answer them for me.

From "Frat" House to Bible School

Now, you would have to know my background to understand how strange it was for me to be reading a book about God. God was the furthest thing from my mind. All that I ever read was what was required of me for school. If I read anything else at all it was *Sports Illustrated*, which I always read from cover to cover. I had never even opened a Bible, much less read one. I just could not get away from what I had seen take place in my father's life. It made me so curious. I respected my father enough to take his advice and find out what was in that little book.

In college, I lived in a fraternity house, or "frat" house as they are commonly called. I don't know how much you have ever heard about fraternity houses, but ours was very typical. It was about a hundred guys all living together in a huge house on the college campus.

Our main goal in life was to see how much beer we could consume on any one given night and still be able to make it to class the next morning. We lived for the weekends when we could party non-stop for two days. I didn't party nearly as much as the others, but I did my fair share. It was in the middle of all this so-called "fun" that I started reading that little book.

The book was about the subject of prayer. It explained the different kinds of prayer that were found in the Bible. I was understanding it just fine until it started mentioning "praying in other tongues." I had never heard of that before. What was this "praying in the Holy Ghost"?

I started looking things up in the Bible for the very first time. I began checking scripture references to see if any of this "praying in tongues" stuff was really in there. I don't even know why I had a Bible at school; I guess my mother had packed it for me. So, I began to look up the scriptures. Sure enough, there it was, right in the New Testament. It had been there the whole time!

DRUNK ON THE HOLY GHOST

I will never forget the night I was filled with the Holy Ghost for as long as I live.

It was a special night in our fraternity. We were having a big party. We had invited a house full of sorority girls over for a crazy spring bash. Every room in the house was decked out for the occasion.

The basement of our house was made up like a disco. We had it all! There was a huge dance floor, a mirrored ball, a bar, and rock music so loud you couldn't hear yourself think. The movie "Saturday Night Fever" and disco dancing were sweeping across America at the time. Being only 5'5", I jokingly say that the only thing I miss about the disco era is the six-inch platform shoes.

I had been reading the book my father gave me for over two weeks now. I kept thinking about all this "speaking with other tongues." stuff. I wondered what it really meant. Scriptures about the "baptism of the Holy Ghost and fire" kept going through my head. That book on prayer was messing up my life! As I sat in class, it seemed all I could think about was the Holy Ghost and praying in the Holy Ghost. I wondered just *what* was this "power from on high" that Jesus said He wanted to give me (Luke 24:49, Acts 1:8). That little book explained it from the bible. It showed me that when you were filled with the Holy Ghost you received supernatural power and you could supernaturally pray in other tongues. It showed me that this experience was for all believers. I was shocked. It was all over the Bible (Acts 2:4, Jude 20, I Corinthians 14). I wondered why no one in my main-line denominational church had told me about this before.

I went to the party that night at our frat house. About halfway through I found myself, beer in hand, dancing with a young lady. I was supposed to be dancing and having a good time, but all I could think about was this Holy Ghost stuff. It was stirring on the inside of me. I told you that book was messing up my life!

Right in the middle of dancing with a girl, without thinking, I stopped moving, looked up, and said out loud to the Lord: "Boy, there has to be more to life than this!" I thought that there must be more than partying, drinking, and trying to have a good time. There just had to be *more* than that. So I walked off and left that poor girl standing there. My mind was so full of what I had been reading and God was tugging on my heart so strong that I left that girl right in the middle of the dance floor. To this day I don't know what happened to her. All I knew was that I had to go talk to God and I had to do it right then.

I went up to my bedroom on the third floor of the fraternity house. I picked up my Bible in one hand and I had that little book in the other. I read that book one more time. When I finished, I said with child-like faith, "Lord, if this Holy Ghost is for real, then I want it! And I want it right now!"

I had never seen anyone filled with the Holy Spirit. I had never heard anyone speak with other tongues, nor had I ever been in a full-gospel, charismatic-type service in my life. All I knew was what Jesus said in Luke 11:9-13. He said that anyone asking for the gift of the Holy Spirit would receive it. I had read about it, I believed it, and now, I *wanted* it.

The music was playing so loud in the basement that night that it was rattling my third-floor window. Remember, I had also been drinking a little bit, but thank God for Matthew 6:33. It says, "They who hunger and thirst after righteousness shall be filled."

When the prayer from my heart went up to God, I sensed something begin to happen on the inside of me. I could feel a presence and power like I had never felt before. My jaw and my lips began to quiver. The next thing I knew I was speaking in this strange language right there in my room! It was bubbling up from inside and it seemed like a river of life was flowing out of me.

Wow! I had been filled with the mighty Holy Ghost. What joy filled my heart! Somehow I knew my life would never be the same. At that moment I did not know that the Lord was going to have me preaching His Gospel all around the world. I just knew that I had received something wonderful and that I would never be the same again.

My Desires and Directions Begin to Change

Not everyone is called to preach in a pulpit or to full-time ministry. However, God does have a wonderful plan for each of us. He has plans to direct your life in the way He knows you should go. He knows the ways that will be a blessing to you and the ways that will also make you a blessing to others. When you are filled with the Holy Ghost and begin to pray in other tongues, the Holy Ghost begins to supernaturally lead you in line with God's plan for your life (Romans 8:26-27).

When I was filled with the Holy Ghost, I found my desires began to change, but it didn't happen overnight like it did for my wife. When Cindy was saved and baptized in the Holy Ghost, she experienced a dramatic change. Immediately, the drugs and the drinking stopped. The cigarettes went out the window. She was instantly a different person. It was a little different for me. My desires changed gradually over the next few months.

You may think or feel that you have to straighten out all the wrong things in your life before God will fill you with the Holy Ghost, but that just simply is not true. The Holy Spirit is a gift from God (Luke 11:13). A gift is not something you work for, earn, or deserve. It is not a reward. Jesus said that the Holy Spirit is a *gift*. God wants to fill you with the Holy Ghost first, and then that new power living on the inside of you will help strengthen you to live right. He will enable you to be the Christian God wants you to be. He will change you from the inside and it will affect your outside.

The Bible says in Matthew 3:11 that when Jesus baptizes you with the Holy Ghost you are filled with the Holy Ghost and fire. What does this fire do?

First, it helps burn up all the chains of sin in your life. I jokingly say Cindy must have had a bonfire when she got filled.

Everything burned off and she was changed instantly. Mine took a little longer to burn everything away, but God began to change my lifestyle into one that glorified Him.

The fire also helps set you ablaze with the power of God. It sets you on fire to be a witness like never before. Jesus said in Acts 1:8 that you would receive power from the Holy Ghost to be a witness for Him. That is exactly what the baptism of the Holy Ghost will open up for you! God's power will flow through you, and make you a tremendous blessing to other people.

His Desires Become My Desires

I didn't know any Spirit-filled Christians. There was no one that I could have fellowship with. It was really amazing how the Lord began to supernaturally lead me as I was reading through the Bible. The Holy Spirit became my teacher. I began to change as I prayed in the Holy Ghost and spent time fellowshipping with the Lord and His Word. Even the way I talked began to change. I found myself not wanting to go to the places I had previously gone to, and not wanting to do the things I used to do. I used to drink, dance, and party as much as I wanted to. Now, I just did not have the "want to" anymore. I loved God too much now. I began to know Him like never before. The Holy Spirit was doing the work in me from the inside out. He was changing my desires and changing me to do God's will.

All of my life the only desire I had was to be a professional trumpet player. Now other things were becoming much more important. I began witnessing for the Lord and praying for others to be filled with the same Holy Spirit and power that I had received. I should warn you here to be careful praying for others to be filled with the Holy Spirit. It is addictive! If you ever lay your hands on someone and they get filled with the Holy Ghost or healed, you will quickly get addicted to doing that all the time. It is so much fun and a thrill like no other. The excitement of God's power flowing through you to bless someone else will change your life forever.

Over the next year and a half, I changed. Reading my Bible and praying in the Holy Ghost allowed the Lord to mold His desires and plans into my heart. I longed to find out God's will for my life. I wanted to do His will more than anything. By December 1979, I had moved to Tulsa, Oklahoma to attend Bible school and I was never to be the same again.

Chapter Two
Are Tongues for Today?

Praying in the Holy Ghost has revolutionized my life.

I grew up in a small Midwestern town and attended one of those "First Church of the Frozen Chosen." Many of you know what I'm talking about. This denomination always tried to skip over what Jesus said in Mark's gospel:

> *"Go ye into all the world, and preach the gospel*
> *to every creature... And these signs shall follow*
> *them that believe... In My name... they shall*
> *speak with new tongues."*
>
> *(Mark 16:15-17)*

It was sad because one of the things my denomination tried to minimize was that Jesus said, "...In My Name... they shall speak with new tongues." They tried to take the miraculous out of God's Word and neutralize everything.

This church taught that God just gave some people the supernatural ability to learn how to speak foreign languages very quickly so that they could go to the foreign mission field and preach the Gospel to people who needed to hear about Jesus. I have been in the ministry for over 40 years now. I have traveled to 32 different countries of the world, and it has never happened like that one time. I often wish it would when I can't speak the language, but I have never gotten it to work that way yet. Not once!

What was Jesus saying in Mark's gospel? Was the "new tongues" He spoke about a language to communicate with another man or was it something different? Well, let's look at that.

"For he that speaketh in an unknown tongue speaketh not unto men, but unto God..." (1 Corinthians 14:2a).

That sort of blows their theology out of the water, doesn't it? Why couldn't these people embrace speaking in tongues as part of the Bible? Why couldn't they see it as the great blessing that God intended for our use today? I believe it's because they were "drunk on religion."

Don't Be Drunk on Religion

Religion has nothing to do with being a Christian. A lot of people are "religious," but they don't know Jesus as their Savior. "Religious" folks have their own ideas about God. The way they judge life and see life is not the way that God sees life. There's a perfect example of this in one of the Old Testament accounts about the children of Israel.

"But they also have erred through wine and strong drink are out of the way; the priest and the prophet have erred through strong drink, they are swallowed up of wine, they are out of the way through strong drink; they err in vision, they stumble in judgment. For all tables are full of vomit and filthiness, so that there is no place clean."

"Whom shall he teach knowledge? And whom shall he make to understand doctrine? Them that are weaned from milk, and drawn from the breasts."

*"For precept must be upon precept, precept upon precept;
line upon line, line upon line; here a little and there a little:*

*For with stammering lips and another tongue will he
speak to these people? To whom he said, 'This is the rest
wherewith ye may cause the weary to rest; and this is
the refreshing: yet they would not hear.'"*

Isaiah 28:7-12

This particular passage tells us the people had wandered away from God and the things of God. The Lord had to raise up the prophet Isaiah to preach to them and get these people to turn from unbelief and sin back to His ways.

One day Isaiah had taken just about all of the hypocrisy and "religiosity" that he could stand. In Isaiah 28:7, He begins to prophesy about religious hypocrites:

*"But they [the religious people] also have erred through
wine and strong drink are out of the way; the priest and
the prophet have erred through strong drink: they are
swallowed up of wine, they are out of the way through
strong drink; they err in vision, they stumble in judgment."*

Isaiah was talking about being drunk. Yes, on alcohol, but I believe he was talking about being "drunk on religion" as well. What does that mean? It means they were consumed with their own religious ideas. When you're drunk on alcohol you're consumed with, or full of alcohol, right? These people were consumed with religious thinking and religious ways. It affected their judgment.

Notice they "erred in vision" and they "stumbled in judgment." They didn't see life the way God sees life. They judged things by denominational teachings, false cults, false religions, or some other way of thinking. These people had gotten away from God and the things of God. Isaiah said they erred in vision, stumbled in judgment, and that they were "drunk on religion."

Let me give you an example of what a person is like who is drunk on religion. Take the subject of divine health for example. The Bible clearly teaches that God still heals today and that Jesus bore our sicknesses. Jesus wants to heal people of sickness today. You might talk to a person who needs healing in their body, and quote scriptures like Psalm 103:2-3 which says:

> *"Bless the Lord, O my soul, and forget not all his benefits: Who forgiveth all thine iniquities; who healeth all thy diseases...."*

Oddly enough some of them will respond by saying, "Well that's not the way *our* church teaches it."

You might say this... "But look at what God's Word says He wants to do. See what it says in Mark 16:16-17: *These signs shall follow them that believe...in my name...they shall lay hands on the sick, and they shall recover...* Please, let me pray with you! I believe God still heals today. He's the same 'yesterday, today, and forever. (Hebrews 13:8)"

And then you may hear something like this... "My grandmother was a very good Christian, and she didn't believe like that. My church doesn't say that. I think I'm just going to stay with my old way of thinking."

That is the way people drunk on religion think. They err, and they stumble. They are consumed with their way of thinking and seeing things. They do not listen to God's Word. They are consumed with error and will not listen to God's Word or His ways.

Finding and Following God's Plan for Your Life

Isaiah points out that there are two ways to learn God's plan for your life:

1.) Do what God says to do and be in His Word.
2.) Pray in the Holy Ghost.

Isaiah said the very first thing that must be established in our lives is the importance of God's Word. Notice what Isaiah says in verse nine about learning the ways of God:

*"Whom shall he [God] teach knowledge? And whom
"shall he [God] make to understand doctrine? Them that
are weaned from the milk, and drawn from the breasts."*

At an early age, you can begin to teach your children about God and His Word. Teach your children to obey *your* voice, and then when they are older they will obey God's voice.

When you discipline their flesh for them and teach them right from wrong, they will be able to do it for themselves when they're grown. Then when they are old, they won't depart from God's ways (Proverbs 22:6). The reason some people have trouble being disciplined and keeping their fleshly desires under control is because their parents did not help them with it when they were small. We must help them discipline their flesh as well as our own.

In the next verse, Isaiah gives us some more instructions: "Precept must be upon precept; line upon line…" (Isaiah 28:10). He's talking about learning the ways of God from the Word of God by reading the Bible.

What does God's Word say you should do? When you don't know what God's will is, start reading your Bible, God's Word. That's the first place you should go to! Go to God's Word. The more familiar you become with the Word of God, the more revelation you will walk in. When you walk in the light of God's Word, His plan will become clearer and easier for you to follow.

Those religious folks didn't put any value on the Word of God. They didn't see that it was actually God speaking to them. If you want solid doctrine, if you want to know the ways of God and what God wants you to do in life, realize that God's Word, your Bible, is *God* speaking to you. It is His personal letter written right to you!

God's Word has instructions for leading us in every area of our lives. You can become a great spouse and parent through His instruction. There's all kinds of information about employer/ employee relationships in the Bible. It is full of practical insight and the blessings of living for God. Everything Jesus paid for is ours if we will read the Word of God. We can find out how to walk in faith and receive all of our inheritance in Christ. Thank God for His Word!

More Revelation About the Plan of God for Your Life

Then, Isaiah begins to prophesy about the second step to learning about God's ways: by praying in the Holy Ghost. This is the very first place in the Bible that I know of that talks about praying in other tongues. He is prophesying about the day in which you and I live. We know this because the Apostle Paul quoted this Old Testament verse in 1 Corinthians 14. That is a New Testament chapter that gives an in-depth understanding of prophecy and speaking with other tongues.

"For with stammering lips and another tongue will he [God] speak to his people." To whom he said, 'This is the rest wherewith ye may cause the weary to rest: and this is the refreshing: yet they would not hear.'"

Isaiah 28:11-12

"Yet they would not hear." "They" who? "They" are the religious folks. It has been about 2,000 years since the outpouring of the Holy Ghost on the day of Pentecost and religious folks still don't like to hear about "speaking in other tongues." Centuries have passed and there is still an element of the church that does not believe or want to hear.

Spiritual Rest and Refreshing

Notice Isaiah said it would be a *rest*. It is a spiritual "refreshing." There have been many times when the pressures or problems of life seem to pull on me. They seem to be closing in all around me.

I'm sure you have been there as well. During those times I like to find scriptures that promise provision for what I need.

I find scripture and I begin to confess them and claim them over my life. Then, I start praying in the Holy Ghost. What refreshment begins to come! What peace begins to flood over my soul! It truly is a rest. It truly is a spiritual "refreshing." The Holy Ghost begins to strengthen my heart and my inner man. He encourages me to go on believing in God's Word. Peace begins to flood my heart and mind. I begin to see and talk victory, hallelujah! It is the best relief for stress that I know.

Praying in tongues will strengthen and refresh your inner man. When your inner man is refreshed it will flow into every area of your life. Thank God for praying in the Holy Ghost!

Chapter Three

Pray in the Holy Ghost
And Pray Out Your Future

I want to lay a foundation for you from God's Word about praying in the Holy Ghost. I also want to give you some practical experiences of "praying out" your future. You will see how to hook up with the Holy Ghost to pray out God's plan for your life.

"For he that speaketh in an unknown tongue speaketh not unto men, but unto God: for no man understandeth him; howbeit in the spirit he speaketh mysteries"

(1 Corinthians 14:2).

This verse says we are not speaking to men but unto God. If you ever get a hold of that revelation you will shout for a week! You are talking directly to God. You are in communication with the one who created the heavens, the earth, and everything in them.

There are people today trying to contact God in all kinds of ways. Some worship cows kiss fat Buddha statues, recite Hare Krishna chants, and others shave their heads. They believe this will bring them closer to God. Do you know why? Because we are all born with a desire to know God our Father. We were designed to draw closer to Him. There is such a hunger in all of mankind to know Him, that we will try anything.

My dear friend, there's only one way to get in touch with The Almighty God. He is our Father God and has done all of the work to make it easy to come to Him. It is through His Son, Jesus Christ. He made a way for us to know Him. When you make Jesus Christ the Lord of your life, the Bible says you shall be saved.

"That if thou shalt confess with thy mouth the Lord Jesus, and shalt believe in thine heart that God hath raised him from the dead, thou shalt be saved. For with the heart, man believeth unto righteousness; and with the mouth, confession is made unto salvation"

(Romans 10:9-10).

He is the way, the truth, and the life, and then He invites you to be filled with the Holy Ghost and receive His power, according to Acts 1:8 and Acts 2:4. When you receive the Holy Spirit with the evidence of speaking in other tongues, you have access to communicate supernaturally with the God of the universe.

PRAYING DIVINE SECRETS

You can talk to God anytime by praying in the Spirit. The more you pray, the more you will begin to understand God's way of thinking and seeing things. How does that happen? By praying in the Spirit—praying in other tongues. It is so important! Look at the rest of 1 Corinthians 14:2:

"Howbeit in the spirit he speaks mysteries."

Notice the word *mysteries.* One translation says the word *mysteries* means "divine secrets." I like that. Notice they are *divine* secrets. They are things that God knows and they are secrets that are hidden from us. Unless we have divine assistance or divine help, we will not be able to see or understand them. Is God trying to hide them from us? No, He is not. He wants to reveal those secrets, or we could say reveal His will, to us. We must have His divine revelation to know God's plan for our lives. It comes by praying out these mysteries in the Holy Ghost in other tongues.

I believe God is trying to get our attention. He wants to be involved in our everyday lives. There are things God is trying to show His children every day. Some decisions need to be made and steps we need to take. God is trying to reveal His will to you and me all the time.

Do you believe God knows more than you do? Of course, He does! He knows more about your children, your job, your business, the economy, and everything else. He knows every detail of His will for your life. I believe God knows more than we do about any situation we face in life. We ought to get up every morning and say, "Thank You, Lord, for Your direction in my life. Thank You, for leading, guiding me, and speaking to me today." Then, take time to get alone with God. Get into your prayer closet and start praying in the Holy Ghost. When you do that, your situation will take on a new perspective. God will shed some of His light on the matter. You will begin to see and understand things that you would have never known without His help.

There have been many times in my life when I didn't know what to do. As I began to pray in the Holy Ghost, it was as if someone suddenly turned on the light switch. I could see so plainly what I needed to do. Was that a coincidence? No way! That is the supernatural way God helps us when we don't know what to do. Praying in the Holy Ghost will give supernatural illumination to our hearts and minds.

The Bible says we see through a glass darkly. In other words, we don't see everything in life as we should. It is like looking through the bottom of two Coke bottles: You can see things, but everything is fuzzy. That is just the way life seems sometimes. As you pray in the Holy Ghost, the mysteries or divine secrets of God's plan will become clearer.

It's like fine-tuning the adjustment on a pair of binoculars. The more you fine-tune them, the better you can see. The more you pray in the Holy Ghost, the more you will fine-tune your spiritual life. When you pray in the Spirit, you will be able to distinguish the way life really is. You won't stumble over knowing whether something is God's direction or the devil trying to pull you off course. You will know which direction to go in life. Your path will be clearer to you.

Go to the Next Level

When you are praying in the Holy Ghost, you are talking to God about the "mysteries" mentioned in 1 Corinthians 14:2. You are praying about divine secrets. You are praying His will and His plan for your life. You are praying out your future right now. You are praying the things that God knows that you don't know. And guess what? He *wants* you to know it! You need to grab a hold of that truth. God wants *you* to know about His plan for your life.

Thank God! He not only wants you to know His plan for your life, He has given you a way to find it out. You can find His will for your life by praying in the Holy Ghost. That, my friend, is really good news! He's given you the *ability* to pray about *divine secrets* in a brand-new language so that He can reveal His will to you. That is how we get *divine assistance*. That is one way we go to the next level in our Christian walk.

A Charge of Holy Ghost Power

"He that speaketh in an unknown tongue edifieth himself."

(1 Corinthians 14:4)

The word *edify* means "to build up," like you would build up your muscles, or "to charge up," like you would charge up a battery on a car.

I grew up in Illinois and we always had very cold winters. There is a lot of ice and snow that blows across the plains. Sometimes it would be so cold that when we would go out in the morning to start the car, we would discover the battery was dead. There was nothing wrong with that car — the battery just needed a charge.

Often we Christians are just like that car. There's absolutely nothing wrong with us. We are right in the middle of the perfect will of God, doing absolutely everything that God wants us to do. We just need a "Holy Ghost charge" to help us out and strengthen us. We need a charge to encourage us to "keep on keeping on." Praying in the Holy Ghost charges up your spiritual battery.

What can you do when your car battery needs a charge? You find a car with a fully charged battery and hook up to it with jumper cables. This transfers a charge to your battery and your battery is thus recharged — right? Well, when you pray in the Holy Ghost, it is just like hooking up spiritual jumper cables to God. His power and strength will begin to flow into your life and build you back up. He will charge the spirit man on the inside of you supernaturally. He will charge you with His power and fire all over again.

Paul *did* say when you prophesy or preach in a known language you build everyone else up. However, you can't build anyone else up unless you are built up first. If I am not edified, or built up, I can not help or edify someone else. When I pray in the Holy Ghost, I build myself up. Then, after being charged, I can be a greater blessing to someone else.

PRAYING GIVES US BOLDNESS TO ACT

"Beloved, building up yourselves on your most holy faith, praying in the Holy Ghost."

(Jude 20)

This verse did *not* say you build up your faith by praying in the Holy Ghost. We must be careful here. The Bible says, we build up our faith by "hearing the Word of God" (Romans 10:17). Then what is Jude saying?

I like what I heard one minister say. He said, "When you pray in the Holy Ghost, you charge yourself up to act on the faith you've already got." When you pray in the Holy Ghost, it fills you up, builds you up, and charges you up to *act* on God's Word. It helps you do what God's Word tells you to do. Praying in the Holy Ghost makes you bold to act in faith. Why? Because you are in communion with God. You are in fellowship with Him.

I have found after prolonged times of praying in the Holy Ghost that many times something more spectacular would happen in my life and ministry. Someone in a church service would be miraculously healed, or a large number of people would come forward to be saved. It just supernaturally charges you up to do greater things for God.

Peter was a different man after he was filled with the Holy Ghost. He denied Jesus three times before his infilling, but afterward, he came out of the upper room on the day of Pentecost, preaching with boldness. As a matter of fact, 3,000 people were saved that day.

As you develop a life of praying in the Holy Ghost, you will find more supernatural things will begin to happen in your life. You will experience supernatural favor and supernatural wisdom. It may seem like favor and wisdom follow you everywhere you go. People will begin to notice a change in you.

Mount Up With Wings As Eagles

"Hast thou not known? Hast thou not heard, that the everlasting God, the Lord, the Creator of the ends of the earth, fainteth not, neither is weary? There is no searching of his understanding" (Isaiah 40:28).

What good news! God never faints, never gets weary, and never runs out of knowing exactly what to do. One thing you will never hear God say is "Uh-oh!" Isn't it encouraging to know you'll never get yourself into any situation that would make God look over the banister of heaven and say, "Oh, no, what am I going to do? Look what they've gotten into now!"

No, a thousand times, no! God is well able to deliver you out of the hand of the enemy. The Bible says that God sits on the throne of heaven and laughs. What is He laughing at? He is laughing at the plans of the devil. The devil actually thinks he can stop God from completing His plan in your life. Here is the good news, God just laughs at him. You might as well laugh at the devil too!

Maybe your situation looks bad. You might say, "That's great, but I'm just about to faint. I want to give up!"

"He giveth power to the faint" (Isaiah 40:29).

This promise is just for you. You might think it's too late. Maybe you've already thrown in the towel. Look at the rest of verse 29:

"And to them that have no might he increaseth strength."

Glory to God! Even if your strength is gone, God will give you His strength to go on.

"Even the youth shall faint and be weary, and the young men shall utterly fall" (Isaiah 40:28).

When you think of young men, what do you think? I think of guys who are in good shape and young men who can go the distance. No matter how strong we may be physically, or how strong we may be mentally, we all face situations sooner or later that our own strength and ability cannot get us out of. Maybe you are there right now. Take heart! Do not feel bad about yourself. We have all been there. It is just a good opportunity for God to prove His Word in your life. Now look at the next verse and get ready to shout!

A Transfer of Strength

"But they that wait upon the Lord shall renew their strength; they shall mount up with wings as eagles; they shall run, and not be weary; and they shall walk, and not faint" (Isaiah 40:31).

When we wait upon the Lord our strength is renewed. The word *renew* in Hebrew means "to change." Within the context of this passage, it means "to exchange." When we wait upon the Lord, we exchange our strength. For what? Why did Isaiah describe to us that God never faints or gets weary, or never runs out of understanding? Well, it is because of this principle: When we wait upon the Lord, we exchange our strength for God's strength, our ability for His ability, and our wisdom for His wisdom. Now that's good news for the weary! As you spend time waiting upon the Lord, there is a divine exchange that takes place. God's strength will begin to flow into your life. You will begin to operate in the wisdom of God. Your strength is exchanged for His strength.

What does it mean to wait upon the Lord? At one time I thought it was just meant to go sit down in the corner somewhere and wait for God to come bail me out of my problems. That can not be right, because Jesus already came 2,000 years ago, and bailed us all out at the cross and the resurrection. He paid the price for our victory once and for all. He never has to conquer defeat for you again. He is the answer to *every* problem.

In 2 Peter 1:3, it says, "His divine power has already given us all things that pertain unto life and godliness." As far as God is concerned, victory has already been purchased for us. But how do we get this victory? We get it by waiting upon the Lord.

When you sit down to eat at a restaurant, who comes up to your table? A waiter or waitress does, right? What are they there for? They are there to take your order and your instructions concerning what you want to eat. That is exactly what it means to wait upon the Lord. It means to go to God and get His instructions about your life and your situation. God always has the answer. He always knows what to do. As you spend time in prayer and fellowship with Him, His plan will be revealed to you. He will show you what to do. You will get His plan, His instruction, and His strength in His presence.

When I get fresh insight and direction it always charges me up. It creates a drive on the inside of me to go do what God wants me to do.

You may already be doing what God wants you to do, but as you wait upon Him, fresh oil from heaven will come and fill you. You will receive fresh strength to run your race for God.

Who's Really Praying - You or the Holy Ghost?

"For if I pray in an unknown tongue, my spirit prayeth, but my understanding is unfruitful." 1 Corinthians 14:14

This verse makes it very clear. It simply means your mind doesn't understand *what* you are praying for when you are praying in the Spirit. Your mind is unfruitful. As you pray in the Holy Ghost, your prayer is not coming from your mind, it is coming from your spirit. Your prayers are not generated by your mind when you pray in the Holy Ghost. This is not something from the mental realm. This is spiritual.

Your mind will tell you that praying in the Holy Ghost is nuts. It will tell you that you are crazy. Oftentimes when you have been praying for a few minutes, your mind will remind you of ten different things you need to do or tell you that you are wasting your time. Your mind will talk to you. Your mind has a voice. If you don't think so, lay down in bed at night after you've had a very busy day, and listen to your mind. It may seem like it is running a million miles an hour and never will stop.

Not only does your mind have a voice, but your body has a voice as well. Just pray for a while and your body will say,

"Hmm, I noticed some leftover chicken in the refrigerator a while ago. Oh, yes, and there is also some of that good potato salad right next to it. You are hungry. Let's go eat and let's do it now!"

Your body may also say, "Hey, let's sit down while we pray. Take it easy!" So you sit down for a couple of minutes and the next thing you know you're hearing, "Hmm, let's just lay down over there... Let's just lay before the Lord and rest in His presence...now close your eyes." Then before you know it, you're not praying anymore. The Lord then has to speak to you in a dream to wake you up. Now, that is funny!

The good news is that our spirit also has a voice! If you pray long enough and stay focused, your mind and body will cry uncle. They will become quiet. Then you will become sensitive to the river of living water that's being produced as you are praying in the Holy Ghost. It will start flowing up from the inside of you right out of your spirit. As you pray, you will get in tune with the voice of your spirit. The more you pray, the more familiar you will become with that voice. Praying in tongues will build up your spirit. The overflow from your time of praying in other tongues will saturate every area of your life.

GET READY TO SHOUT

"My spirit (by the Holy Spirit within me) prays" (1 Corinthians 14:14 AMP).

Notice what verse 14 says. It says that it is *your spirit* doing the praying. I like what the amplified Bible says: "My spirit (by the Holy Spirit within me) prays." On the day of Pentecost when they were all filled with the Holy Ghost, it says they *all* began to speak with other tongues as the "Holy Ghost gave them utterance."

Notice the Holy Ghost is giving the utterance, or the language, or the words to speak in prayer. He is making up the prayer. It is the job of the Holy Ghost to help you pray! He is the one who hooks up with you. He takes hold together with you. He is the one helping you to pray out those divine secrets. He gives you the utterance, but *you* are still doing the "praying." He is praying through you even though you don't understand the language. We are so limited in our minds to only know what we know and see what we can see in this natural world. The Holy Spirit is not limited. He knows everything. He is the one helping you to pray.

God is so smart. I am convinced that if we did know and understand all that we were praying about, many times we would surely mess it up. We would try to make things happen out of the Lord's timing. God has really helped us here. He designed a supernatural way that He can pray for us when we don't even know what to pray for as we ought to know.

> *"Likewise the Spirit also helpeth our infirmities: for we know not what we should pray for as we ought: but the Spirit itself maketh intercession for us with groanings which cannot be uttered.*
>
> *And he that searcheth the hearts knoweth what is the mind of the Spirit, because he maketh intercession for the saints according to the will of God." (Romans 8:26-27)*

THE BEST PART YET

When the Holy Ghost helps us to pray, it is a perfect prayer. He knows what we are missing. He knows exactly what each one of us needs. Now, here's the shouting part: It is not the Holy Ghost talking to God the Father—it is YOU! The Holy Ghost, as you pray in the Spirit, is giving *you* just what needs to be said in prayer, and giving you what to ask Him for. In other words, He is praying God's divine will through you by praying in the Holy Ghost, yet *you* are the one doing the praying.

I am so thankful that God bypasses the limitations of our minds when we don't know what to pray for in situations. We may not know what we are praying about with our minds when we are praying in the Spirit. That doesn't stop God's ability to be able to answer that prayer even though your mind doesn't know what you are asking for or praying about. The Holy Ghost is making up the prayer, but *you* are the one who is asking; therefore God has a divine right to answer that prayer. He can now bring it to pass in your life. Even though you don't know exactly what you are praying for, He receives it, and can now answer it. Glory to God!

When you need help with a business decision, your children, your marriage, or anything, praying in the Holy Ghost helps you pray the perfect will of God over your situation. God now has the legal right to intervene and cause things to go your way. Legally, He can bring His will to pass because you are the one actually asking Him for it. You have prayed out His perfect will and plan when you pray in the spirit. Even though your mind doesn't know exactly what you prayed, He does. It was His perfect will. Wow! Our God is so good!

ANOTHER BENEFIT OF PRAYING IN TONGUES

"Likewise, the Spirit also helpeth our infirmities."
(Romans 8:26 KJV)

The word *infirmities* in the original Greek text means "tests, trials, afflictions, weaknesses, and limitations." It can also literally mean sickness and disease. I like to put it this way as well: An infirmity is our inability to get the job done. Notice that it says the Holy Spirit helps us in those tests, trials, afflictions, weaknesses, and limitations.

Now read the next line: "For we know not what we should pray for as we ought." It did not say that we didn't know *how* to pray. It just says there are times when we do not know *what* to pray for as we ought. While you may not know *what* to pray for, you do know *how* to pray. We pray in the Holy Ghost and He makes intercession for us with groanings that cannot be uttered. That is speaking in other tongues.

There have been times in my life when it seemed like the answers I needed just weren't there. I had followed the "ten steps to victory" principles as best I could, but it still didn't seem like anything was working. Have you ever been there? I was doing my best. I was doing everything in the Word of God that I knew to do at the time, but for some reason, it did not seem like victory was knocking on my door the way it should have.

Oh, thank God for Ephesians 6:13,14: "And having done all, to stand. Stand, therefore…"

One of the best ways to "stand" is to pray in the Holy Ghost.

Ask the Holy Ghost to help you in your test, your trial, and your infirmity. Greek scholars tell us that the word *help* means that the Holy Ghost will "take hold together with you against" the test or the trial.

Thank God, you are not in this life alone. You don't have to make business decisions at work all by yourself. You are not helplessly dealing with situations concerning your children. You do not have to face marriage problems in your own strength and wisdom. Thank God! The Holy Ghost wants to take hold together with you. As you yield to the Holy Ghost, He will pray His perfect will through you. He will strengthen you. Glory to God!

How does He do all of this? Let's look once more at Romans 8:26-27:

> *"For we know not what we should pray for As we ought: but the Spirit itself maketh intercession for us with groanings which cannot be uttered.*

(One translation Says "in articulate speech." That is praying in other tongues.)

> *"And he that searcheth the hearts knoweth what is the mind of the Spirit, because he maketh intercession for the saints according to the will of God."*

Did you know that the Holy Ghost knows right where you fit into the plan of God? He knows exactly what you are supposed to be doing. He knows where you are hitting it, and where you are missing it. He knows where you need help. As you pray, He will get you smack-dab into the middle of the will of God for your life. He will help you.

I've heard some of the wildest "revelations" come out of verse 27. Some people just get super "spooky," spiritually speaking. Have you ever met anybody like that? They read that verse like this: "The mind of the Spirit" and try to make it say something other than what it means. Ultimately, the phrase "mind of the Spirit" is just an old Elizabethan term from King James English. Unfortunately, it has mixed some people up.

I remember how often my grandmother used the term "mind." She would say, "You know, I've got a mind to go to the post office this morning," or, "I've got a mind to go visit our relatives over in such and such a city." She had a "mind" to do this, or a "mind" to do that. What was she saying? She was saying that she had a *plan*. That is exactly what this old Elizabethan term means. The word *mind* means *"plan."* The Holy Ghost knows exactly where you fit into the plan of God. The Holy Ghost will make intercession for you according to the mind of the Spirit, or the plan of God for your life.

God has a perfect plan for your life. It's a place of peace, provision, life, joy, health, and even prosperity. When you are walking in God's perfect plan, you are in that place. It truly is a place of blessing.

OUR GUIDE — THE HOLY GHOST

Just because you are in the perfect plan of God, that does not mean that there won't be tests and trials. Someone once asked me in the middle of a difficult test, "How can you have a smile on your face when you're going through something like that?" I answered, "Because no matter how high the waves may get, or how hard the wind may blow, I know Jesus is in my boat. I am going to the other side. The Holy Ghost is in me and He is taking hold together with me. Praise God! He knows the plan of God for my life, and I am trusting Him. He is leading me through the storm to victory."

The Holy Ghost is called our guide. If you hired a guide to lead you through the mountains, he would show you the best way to go. He has more experience. He knows every detail of the route. He shows you the best route to take and shows you where there may be problems. He does not force you to follow; He leads you in the right direction. It is up to you to listen and follow His instructions.

God never said there wouldn't be any mountain passes to traverse. God never said that there would not be any tests or hard places to go over. The good news is that you have the guide — the Holy Spirit — on the inside of you. He knows the best way to go. He knows every detail of the plan to get you to your perfect destination. When we pray in the Spirit, He takes hold together with us and helps us pray down the plan of God right into our midst. He will let you know the right way to go. He will strengthen your spirit man as you pray in the Holy Ghost. You will sense His strength begin to carry you through.

"And he that searcheth the hearts knoweth what is the mind of the Spirit." (Romans 8:27)

Notice the word "hearts" is plural. As the Holy Spirit wills, you can pray for other people by praying in tongues. Sometimes you will know who you are praying for and you may even get a sense of what it is about. Other times you may not know who it was for or what it was for. You may not know the good you did until you get to heaven and receive your reward. Those of us who preach think we are going to receive great rewards because of what we see happening in our services. I believe that the prayer team has a lot to do with the victories we see in services. Someday in heaven, the Lord is going to show us what the prayer team in that church accomplished. Yes, we will get our reward, but so will everyone who prayed out the plan of God. They opened a door in the supernatural so that He could move and do what He wanted to do. What a thrill to get to work with the mighty Holy Ghost!

Chapter Four

Avoid Danger and Tragedy by Praying in the Holy Ghost

One time while ministering overseas in Europe, I had an outstanding experience happen to me in prayer. It didn't seem like it at the time, but later I learned that my brother's life had been spared.

I go through a routine every morning. About the time I get in the shower to start getting ready for the day, I usually start praying and just fellowshipping with the Lord.

Time is such a precious commodity. Everyone's schedule is so hectic. A lot of times I hear people say they cannot find the time to pray. I have found that we can rearrange and reevaluate some of our activities and pray in the Holy Ghost while doing other things. We can pray in the Spirit while on the way to work, on the way home from work, getting ready in the morning, mowing the grass, or anything a person does in their daily routine. If you ask the Lord to help you, He will show you ways and times that you can pray in the Spirit while you are doing something else.

To continue with my story, this particular morning I got into the shower and started my daily routine. I started quoting various scriptures and talking to the Lord about some things that I was believing Him for. I claimed the promises of God and reminded Him of His Word. I began to worship the Lord a little bit and pray in the Holy Ghost. That is part of my normal daily routine. This morning, the moment I stepped out of the shower, these English words came up out of my spirit and then out of my mouth: "Devil, take your hands off my brother in the Name of Jesus."

I have a brother who is a band director in Illinois. He is a good man and we have always loved each other greatly. To be honest with you, however, I had not thought about him in weeks. Traveling ministry kept Cindy and me very busy and I knew that he was safe and sound working there in Illinois. The Holy Ghost must have had me praying for my brother. I was on the other side of the world getting ready for my day, minding my own business. Thank God there is no distance in the Spirit, or in prayer. I thought, *Wow! That was interesting.* I had to preach three classes in a Bible school that morning, so I went ahead and started thinking about what I was going to be teaching and just forgot about it.

It was about three more weeks before we got back home to the States. Being the good son that I am, after a good night's sleep, I promptly called my mother to see how she was doing. We were right in the middle of our conversation when she suddenly interrupted me, "Oh Bruce! You didn't hear what happened to your brother while you were gone, did you? His car caught on fire and completely blew up!" I said, "Blew up? Mom, what in the world do you mean that his car blew up? He's driving a brand-new car!"

She went on to tell me this amazing story. My brother was coming home from work one day when his brand-new car started to smoke. Well, that's a little unusual for a new car, but he didn't think it was anything serious. The dealership where he purchased it was just a few blocks away, so he decided to drive over to the car lot and see what they had to say.

He had to pass a friend's house while on the way to the dealership. As he did, the thought flashed through his mind:

"Why not stop here and call the dealership and see what they want you to do." Oh, thank God for those thoughts that flash through our minds! Many times, a thought may be coming from our spirit man on the inside. It could be the Lord trying to get our attention. We have not always listened to that still small voice of the Holy Ghost, but we are getting better at it. Praise God! That is where He speaks. The Holy Spirit speaks from the inside, not from the outside.

So, my brother pulled his car over in front of his friend's house and got out. A few seconds later as he walked up the front steps, the car burst into flames. The roof blew off the car and fire completely engulfed the car. He is also a trumpet player, so he had his trumpets with him in the trunk of his car. They were in a fireproof case, but that fire was so intense that it charred the trumpet case.

Oh, thank God for the Holy Ghost! All God was looking for that day as I showered was somebody available to pray. He needed someone to stand in the gap to save my brother's life. I had no idea what was going to happen, but God did. God already had the situation handled through prayer before it happened. Glory to God! My brother was just fine and is living happily on the earth today. Someone asked me one time, "What about the car?" Well, yes, the Lord does care about your things, but that car is a piece of metal that can be replaced. My brother could not be replaced. God can get a new car for us. A human life saved is the most important thing. Thank God for praying in the Holy Ghost! The tragedy the devil had planned for my brother's life was avoided by prayer.

I am thoroughly convinced no matter who you are, and no matter what you do in life, the Holy Ghost will connect with you and help you to pray out the plan of God for your future. Divine protection is just a part of the blessings for the child of God who dwells in the secret place of the Most High in prayer.

If you are a business person, the Holy Ghost will join with you just like He will join with a preacher. If you are a parent, the Holy Ghost will hook up with you to be the best mom or dad you can be. If you are a student or young person, He will help you excel in all that you do. He will lead you and guide you. He will help you supernaturally pray out the plan of God for your life, your family, and the people around you.

Chapter Five
Becoming More Sensitive To God's Voice

I remember when the Lord first put the Rhema Singers & Band together in 1981. Cindy and I had the privilege to travel with the Kenneth Hagin Ministries Crusade Team and the Rhema Singers & Band for about six and a half years. We saw the Lord do so many miraculous things. We witnessed many amazing healings, and lives changed. The truths we learned from the Word of God in the meetings helped to shape and mold us. It set the stage for our whole lives. What an honor it was to serve the Hagins and that ministry! We are so very grateful for that precious time and for all they poured into us.

You may have seen or heard the Rhema Singers & Band after they were fully developed. I was in the very first Rhema Singers & Band in the infancy stage. What they were then is not what they ultimately became. We started out as just a bunch of young kids going to bible school who didn't know very much but were eager to learn. I jokingly say that we would not have recognized the Holy Ghost in a service if He would have walked up and pinched us.

We did not know anything about the moving of the Spirit. Thank God that the Hagins were just like Jesus! They were full of patience. They saw that God was training all of us and helped us to learn. Many times we would get up and sing the wrong song in the service and just quench the anointing. We loved God and had a lot of zeal, but we didn't know how to flow with the Spirit.

I will never forget one particular Winter Bible Seminar at Rhema. This was one of Brother Hagin's biggest meetings of the year. It was the last night, and we wanted to do our very best for God and to serve Brother Hagin. We got up on the platform and (bless our darling hearts), we completely sang the wrong song. It was like pouring water on a fire. It just quenched the anointing. It flew out of there like a bird—tweet, tweet, tweet… GOOD-BYE! We not only *didn't* help Brother Hagin minister, but we also made it very difficult for him to minister at all.

Here is just a thought. The music ministry falls under the "Helps" ministry and is meant to be operated supernaturally. The Lord will work with the natural talent you have and that you have developed. He wants to use it in a very supernatural way. It is a precious thing to have the opportunity to aid and help the ministry gift or gifts where the Lord allows you to serve through music ministry. How do you know what the right song is that you should sing or play? Well, number one, the right song is a song with *scriptural* and *faith-filled* words. It is a song that will help usher in the presence of God for what He wants to do in that service. The Lord does not want to do the same thing every service. You must find out what direction He is going in for that service and follow Him. The right song will *help* the ministry gift you are there to serve. If it doesn't help the gift of God that you are there to assist, it is the wrong song. It is the song that the Lord *leads* you to sing, not just the one you *like* to sing. It is the right song, at the right time, and when He tells you to sing it. You can sing a really good song at the wrong time–and it is the wrong song. Musicians must be filled and led by the Holy Ghost to be the real help that they are destined to be.

That night at the Winter Bible Seminar, Brother Hagin got up and walked behind the pulpit after we sang. He seemed to just hem-haw around for a little while. It seemed like he was searching for the right way to go. Suddenly he looked up and said, "You know, when the music ministry gets to the place that it ought to be, then you will see the prophet's ministry get to the place that it ought to be."

I thought to myself, *Do you think he might be talking about us?* Sure he was! We knew that we were not where we needed to be, but we really did not know how to get there. So, we did what we knew to do. What we knew to do was to pray in the Holy Ghost. We were hearing the good Word of God taught all the time in school at RHEMA, but we knew we needed to pray in the Holy Ghost to help us become more sensitive to the voice of the Spirit.

We talked about it and we all decided that we as a group, the Rhema Singers & Band, would get together after work and spend time in prayer. We wholeheartedly wanted to learn the ways of the Holy Spirit. We so wanted to be a help to Brother Hagin and not a hindrance. You know it's serious if young people are getting together to pray on their own. We would all cram into a little house where some of the group lived and begin to seek God. The Lord met us there and we had some of the most extraordinary experiences in prayer. As we started spending that extra time in His presence praying in the Holy Ghost, the glory of God would come in and absolutely fill that house. The power of God immersed us in that place.

One night we were praying, and the power of God filled the room so much that our piano player fell out. I don't mean he just fell like you would trip or faint. The power of God was so strong that he went out in the Spirit. When the Lord fills a room or comes upon a person in a strong way, something must give! It is not going to be the Power of God that gives. The anointing is real. It is like electricity. Many times, your flesh will fall under the anointing and power of God.

Well, when our piano player fell out, he hit his head on the corner of a wall. It sounded just like a cannon going off. KABOOM! We thought he had really hurt himself. We wondered if we were going to have to raise him from the dead like the man who fell out of the window when Paul was preaching. We all kept praying and watching to see what would happen next. When this piano player finally came to himself, he sat up and said, "Glory to *God!*" He had an experience in the presence of the Lord. He didn't even know that he hit his head on the wall–he did not even feel it! He said it felt like he fell into a cloud of cotton balls. He said that the Lord ministered to him and spoke to him in a very special way while he was on the floor in His presence.

It was absolutely astounding! Things began to happen in those prayer meetings. Supernatural things began to happen as we prayed. Among other things, during that time, Cindy and I began to date. It may not have blessed anyone else, but it sure did bless us! Hallelujah! I can't think of a better place to find a godly mate, and a match made in heaven, than in the presence of God!

In His presence, you can hear and learn to follow His lead. We continued coming together as a group and praying. We prayed that way for weeks and even months. Even at the very beginning of the times, we set aside to pray, the meetings that we were ministering in began to change. We would get into the services to minister with Brother Hagin and instead of not knowing what to do, we began to *know* what to do. It did not happen all at once, but as we prayed in the Holy Ghost, we became much more sensitive to the voice of God. Let me encourage you, if this will work for musicians, this will work for anybody.

I believe this works for parents with their children! I believe this works with business people in their businesses! I believe this works for any decision that you must make in life and any situation that you face. As you pray in the Spirit, the plan of God will be worked out in your life. It's God's supernatural way of helping you.

GET TO KNOW THE VOICE OF GOD

Did you know it's possible to be born again, love God with all your heart, and still not know God's voice? How do you get to know the voice of God?

There are two ways: The first way is by reading, meditating, and becoming familiar with the Word of God. The same Holy Ghost that lives on the inside of you wrote Matthew, Mark, Luke, and John. If you want to know what the Holy Ghost sounds like, He sounds just like what Matthew, Mark, Luke, and John said in their gospels. The more familiar you get with the written Word of God, the more often you will recognize Him when He speaks to you in that still small voice.

Have you ever been in a situation where you did not know what to do when, all of a sudden, a scripture came back to your remembrance? Guess what? That is the Holy Ghost. It could be a verse from Proverbs or something you heard your pastor say in church on Sunday. It might be something you heard two years ago, and it would behoove you to listen to that. That is the Holy Ghost leading you. That is just as supernatural as raising the dead.

Many times, we are looking for God to lead us spectacularly and the supernatural is there the whole time. It is His Word.

The second way we become familiar with the voice of God is by praying in the Holy Ghost. Praying in other tongues flows right out of your mouth. That's the same place where the Holy Spirit bears witness to your spirit. We call that the inward witness. Your inward man is the same place the river of other tongues comes from. It is your spirit man. The more familiar you get with the river of praying in other tongues, the more familiar you will get with God. It will help you hear the voice of His Spirit whenever and however He speaks.

The more time you spend in the presence of God, the more you will know His voice. Let's say that you heard me speak one time and you never listened to me again for a year. You probably would not recognize my voice if I called you on the phone. Now, if you had some of my teaching series and you listened to them every single day for a whole year, you would most likely recognize my voice when I called. You would know it was me.

It is the same way with God. If you spend time praying in the Holy Ghost, you will become familiar with that precious river. Jesus mentioned this river in John 7:38-39:

> *"He that believeth on me, as the scripture hath said, out of his belly shall flow rivers of living water. But this spake he of the Spirit, which they that believe on him should receive: for The Holy Ghost was not yet given; because that Jesus was not yet glorified."*

Chapter Six
Seasons of Prayer

In 1985, while Cindy and I were still with the Rhema Singers & Band, I went through what I call a "season of prayer." That's the only way I know how to put it. I was just burdened to pray.

There appear to be different times in which we need to pray. First, we pray because we know we love the Lord and we maintain fellowship with Him.. We see it in the Word and desire a relationship with God. We know we need to be disciplined in that area. We need to build up our spiritual batteries and praying in the Holy Ghost charges us up.

Second, we may get a "leading" from the Holy Ghost that we need to pray. It starts as a desire to pray for someone or an event, or we get an inward witness that we just need to pray.

Third, there are times when the desire to pray is so strong that if you don't pray, it seems like you'll explode. You are compelled to pray. That's the way I was praying. I was even skipping meals. Now anyone who knows me could testify that if I am skipping meals to go pray, I have a burden to pray!

We were in the middle of a crusade with Brother Hagin in Richmond, Virginia. I would go to a little prayer room in the convention center. It was the same room where we would take people to be saved and filled with the Holy Ghost when Brother

Hagin would give the altar calls. Whenever we had any extra time, I locked myself in there and then I would walk from one end of the room to the other praying in other tongues.

At that time, I was still relatively new to the things of God. I knew how to pray in tongues, but something different began to happen. I had never experienced anything like this before. While praying in the Holy Ghost, every once in a while, I would speak out a word in English. That word was "East!" It would come right out of the same place that tongues come from. Then I would pray some more in the Holy Ghost. My praying intensified, and so did the word:

"EE-AA-SS-TT!"

It got to the point that no matter if I was praying by myself, or praying with the group, or my wife, here it would come again: "East! East!" I started thinking, *I'm on the East Coast. Maybe God wants us to move here and start a church.* You know, you get into trouble when you try to interpret things with your mind. I wondered if I was just praying for the East Coast because we were there. The next crusade, we were in another part of the United States and I was still praying out the word, *"East."*

Needing some answers, I scheduled an appointment with the head of the prayer ministry for Kenneth Hagin Ministries. This woman is an experienced prayer warrior who has been praying for years. I told her what was happening in my prayer life and she got an excited look on her face. "That's the Holy Ghost!" she exclaimed. "You're praying in tongues and interpreting some of what you're praying in English. Keep praying that until you get through. Don't stop praying until the burden is lifted, and until you have a sense of victory."

That is exactly what I did. I prayed that way for months. I just stuck with it. I prayed what was coming from my heart all the way through until the burden of it lifted off of me. One day I realized I had not been praying about that for a while. I was praying about other things and just went on.

I learned a lot through this experience. It is similar in prayer and the things of the Spirit. You learn from the Word and by example. I can teach you what I know, but prayer is a lot like driving a car. You can learn a lot by sitting in a classroom with a book. However, driving takes on a whole new meaning when you are behind the wheel and put that car into drive. The most wonderful life to be lived is the life of prayer as you are walking in fellowship with God. The exciting part is being able to pray and watch God bring His will and plan to pass in our lives.

On September 17, 1987, Cindy and I left Brother Hagin's ministry and launched our own ministry. Two years after that, we were invited to go to Europe with some good friends who had been ministering over there for years. We were so excited. It had always been in our hearts to help take the gospel to Europe. This trip was extra special because we were going to go to Germany and into East Germany. That was when East Germany still existed. We were to minister in a Bible school where East German pastors were coming to learn the Word of God.

The day finally came to go. We ministered in various parts of Europe and then flew into Berlin. It was so cold that day. It was one of the coldest days I had ever felt in my life. We were going into East Germany through "Checkpoint Charlie" later that night. Politically, things were changing right then, and communism was ready to fall. We heard that the German guards by the Brandenburg Gate were limitedly letting people chip off pieces of the Berlin Wall. Our friends had been going in and out of Eastern Europe for years and they wanted a piece of the Wall. We did too. We borrowed a hammer and chisel from our smll hotel and went out to collect souvenirs.

We arrived and hurriedly began to chip at the concrete wall that had held Eastern Europe captive for so long. As I was chipping away, the Holy Ghost came upon me. He reminded me of all those days I had prayed out, "East! East!" Then it hit me! I said out loud, "Oh, my Lord, this is the East!" 'East' meant Eastern Europe! I'm going into the East. This is what I prayed about! This is the "EAST!" Tears welled up in my eyes and joy filled my heart.

Back in 1985, I was not very familiar with Europe. I did not know you could split Europe right down the middle and that one half of Europe was called the East, and the other half was called the West.

The western side was the free part, and the eastern side of Europe was the part that was under communist rule. I didn't realize that all those days and weeks, I was praying out the plan of God for my life to go minister in Eastern Europe. I know that God had a lot of people praying for the Berlin Wall to come down. Do you know what? I was one of them!

In 1985, no one had any idea that communism would fall and the Eastern Wall was going to come down. I had no idea that we would be able to go into the East and preach the Gospel, but God did. That's why He had people praying. We were able to go back and minister in Eastern Europe many, many times. We met so many precious people. God always seemed to move wonderfully and powerfully every time we would go.

Back at the Berlin Wall in 1989, I knew Cindy and I were walking out the plan of God for our lives. It was the plan that we had prayed out! Oh, hallelujah! You can do that for your life as well.!

As you pray in the Spirit, God will move you into the fullness of His plan. He will guide you to be exactly where He wants you to be! There is no place I'd rather be than in the perfect will of God. How about you? It is a great place to be! He will get all the glory because He is the one who gets us there. We just cooperate with Him by praying out His plan for our lives in other tongues.

Chapter Seven
The Early Church Gets Divine Direction Through Prayer

"Now there were in the church that was at Antioch certain prophets and teachers; such as Barnabas, and Simeon that was called Niger, Lucius of Cyrene, and Manaen, which had been brought up with Herod the Tetrarch, and Saul. As they ministered to the Lord, and fasted, the Holy Ghost said, separate me, Barnabas and Saul, for the work whereunto I have called them. And when they had fasted and prayed and laid their hands on them, they sent them away. So they, being sent forth by the Holy Ghost departed." Acts 13:1-4

Here is an instance in scripture where we can learn how to receive direction for our lives from the Holy Ghost. In this passage, certain prophets and teachers assembled together and began to minister to the Lord. Do you know what it means to minister to the Lord? It can mean several things. Some of ministering to the Lord means to pray, to praise, and to sing praises to God. It means taking time to wait on Him. These men of God were ministering to the Lord. In that kind of atmosphere, they received specific direction from the Holy Ghost. Verse two says: "The Holy Ghost said…" He spoke and He told these men what to do.

These preachers, prophets, and teachers could have preached to one another, but they did not come to preach. They came to minister to the Lord and to spend time in God's presence. You will find there are going to be times in your Christian walk when you need to set everything else aside to ascertain the will of God. It helps to make time to get away and lock yourself in with God and His Word. When you need to hear from heaven, direction will come as you minister to the Lord and pray in the Holy Ghost.

I can give you example after example of how the Lord has given me direction in my life, but He wants you to experience hearing from heaven for yourself. Lock yourself in with God. He will reveal himself to you when you seek Him and pray in the Holy Ghost. He will mold your desires to become His desires. You will begin praying out the plan of God. You will begin to know his voice and see what He has ahead for you. Tremendous things will take place in your life.

Here in Acts 13, I am convinced as this company of men set time aside to seek God and pray, it was then that they saw the next piece of the puzzle. It was then that tremendous things got started, or we could say tremendous things were "birthed." The Holy Ghost "said" in that time of prayer, "Separate me Paul and Barnabas for the work that I have called them to." Notice the calling was already there, but time spent waiting on God and praying in the Spirit revealed the plan. Even after the Holy Ghost "said," the disciples prayed some more. They waited on God some more, and *then* they laid hands on them to send them out.

They were separated by the calling of God in those meetings. They prayed, heard from God, and laid hands on them under the direction of the Holy Ghost. There was an anointing from the Holy Ghost that was there to do it. It was more than just a good thought to do a good work. It was divine direction from the Spirit of God for the plan and how to carry out the plan. They were separated by the Holy Ghost to a God-given office in the body. The Holy Ghost sent them forth supernaturally with the anointing and sent them by the anointing. It was not just a plan that someone thought up or a denomination offered. It was THE PLAN OF GOD, and it came about by waiting on God.

When these men gathered to minister to the Lord, no one had been what we would call a "missionary" up to that point. Christianity was basically only in Jerusalem and Antioch. Out of that prayer meeting, the Holy Ghost gave a supernatural commission to Paul and Barnabas to take the Gospel to other places also. The churches of Ephesus, Corinth, and Galatia came out of that prayer meeting. The Colossian, Thessalonian, and Philippian churches were also a result of the works of Paul and Barnabas. Without hearing from the Holy Ghost, Paul, and Barnabas might never have gone to those places with the Gospel. Notice it all started by spending time in prayer. *Good things always come out of a season of prayer.*

There are a lot of really good things that you can do for Jesus. It is good to have a heart for the kingdom and to put your hand to do anything you can for the kingdom of God. The Lord wants to lead you in those areas as well. People think up a lot of good plans, but the best plan is the one that is initiated by God, that you have heard from the Spirit of God. Don't ever do anything just because it is a "good idea" or a lot of people are doing it. Be LED by the Spirit. Get into the word of God and the presence of God, and wait on HIM! The Lord has plans right now for our future, our families, and our course in life. He knows the next step we are to take. Wouldn't it be sad to never know what the plan of God is for our lives? Wouldn't it be sad to just live *hoping* that you are in the will of God? The good news is that He wants us to know! We *can* know and we can be *supernaturally* led to do the will of God in our lives. *A season of prayer brings a season of blessing!*

My Wife Gets a Holy Ghost Plan

Cindy was filled with the Holy Ghost at the altar in a precious little Pentecostal church in Golden, Colorado. They were in the middle of a 60-day revival that would change her life forever.

Every night the services would end by gathering people around the altar to pray. It was during those times of drawing close to God that she says she experienced the move of the Spirit for the first time. People got saved and there were healings during that time. People grew closer to the Lord and had supernatural experiences in prayer. Many times, the presence of God was so strong that they would pray until after midnight and not even be aware of the time. Cindy had a witness on the inside that she was praying out God's will for her life right then and for years to come. Many things have come to pass, and some things are even yet coming to pass that she prayed about during those times at the altar.

She experienced this type of prayer when she was a 17-year-old girl who had just received the baptism of the Holy Ghost. Hearing from God is not limited to age or gender. This is for anyone who will receive and take time to minister to the Lord. The call has gone forth. He wants us to experience His presence. He wants to reveal himself to us. He wants us to walk in His very best.

Chapter Eight
"Easier Caught Than Taught"

Very often things we teach about prayer and the spirit of prayer are "easier caught than taught."

It's sort of like driving a car. You probably learned a lot sitting behind a simulator, reading instruction books, and watching the teacher write on the chalkboard. However, when you actually got in the car with your instructor, you learned a lot more from them by actually sitting next to them. They drove and you watched to see what they did and how they did it. While you watched, you learned—or caught—that from them.

Many times, the things of prayer are exactly the same way. When you get around people who pray, a spirit of prayer will rub off on you. It's a lot like the spirit of faith. I love hanging around people who have the spirit of faith. Why? It rubs off on me! It encourages me to believe in God for more. It encourages me to do more for God. Likewise, when I hang around people who have a spirit of prayer, it makes me want to pray more.

When I was going to Bible school, I always liked going to prayer school in the afternoon. There were always what I call "prayer warriors" there. They were seasoned veterans of prayer. They knew how to hook up with the Holy Ghost and pray out the plan of God.

I watched how they prayed. I listened to how they prayed. I watched what they did. I would just get in that atmosphere of anointing in prayer, and it started getting off on me. It changed me. It made me hungry to pray. Now I wanted to pray out God's plan for my life. I got to know and experience Him in prayer.

I have been saying the spirit of prayer is "easier caught than taught" for years, but I didn't have any scripture to back it up. Now I've got scripture, glory to God! So I am even more bold about it. Let me explain more about that as we look at the Book of Acts.

The church in Antioch had just started and the people were on fire for God. They were doing great things for the Lord. People were being saved by the multitudes. Antioch was having a revival. The church in Jerusalem, however, was under heavy persecution.

"And in these days came prophets from Jerusalem unto Antioch. And there stood up one of them named Agabus and signified by the spirit that there should be great dearth throughout all the world: which came to pass in the days of Claudius Caesar. Then the disciples, every man according to his ability, determined to send relief unto the brethren which dwelt in Judea: (In other words, they took up an offering for the Christians in Jerusalem.) **Which also they did, and sent it to the elders by the hands of Barnabas and Saul."** (Barnabas and Saul were elected to take the money to the church of Jerusalem. Now notice what Barnabas and Saul walked into when they got to Jerusalem.) **"Now about that time Herod the King stretched forth his hands to vex certain of the church. And he killed James the brother of John with the sword. And because he saw it pleased the Jews, he proceeded further to take Peter also. (Then were the days of unleavened bread.) And when he had apprehended him, he put him in prison and delivered him to four quaternions of soldiers to keep him; intending after***

Easter to bring him forth to the people. Peter therefore
was kept in prison: but prayer was made without
ceasing of the church unto God for him." Acts 11:27-12:15

Paul and Barnabas walked into an atmosphere that was filled
with some serious prayer. James had been killed and they had
taken Peter as a prisoner. The church probably figured out that
Peter was to be executed after Easter, so they went to prayer. I
believe the Lord used this as an opportunity to teach Paul and
Barnabas something about united prayer so they could take it
back to the church at Antioch.

What Is Corporate Prayer?

The church at Antioch had a foundation of soul-winning.
They had good teaching, but God wanted to add something else
to them. I'll prove it to you from scripture. Go back to Acts 11:22-
26:

"Then tidings of these things came unto the ears of the
church which was in Jerusalem: and they sent forth
Barnabas, that he should go as far as Antioch. Who,
when he came and had seen the grace of God, was glad,
and exhorted them all, that with the purpose of heart,
they would cleave unto the Lord. For he (Barnabas)
was a good man, full of the Holy Ghost and faith: and
many people were added unto the Lord." (There's the
soul winning!) "Then departed Barnabas to Tarsus, for
to seek Saul: And when he had found him, he brought
him unto Antioch. And it came to pass, that a whole
year they assembled themselves with the church and
[what did they do? They] taught many people. And the
disciples were called Christians first in Antioch."

Notice what is occurring in the church at Antioch. They have
evangelism, and that is very important. When soul winning is

first, other things will begin to fall into place. There is also good teaching. I'm sure Paul and Barnabas were tremendous teachers. The church was grounded in evangelism and teaching, but that's not all there is in a healthy relationship with God.

There is so much more that can be accomplished when we learn how to develop ourselves in prayer. I believe that is one of the reasons God sent Paul and Barnabas to Antioch. He wanted these men to catch the spirit of prayer that rested upon the saints there.

Now, I am not implying that Paul and Barnabas did not pray. I am sure that they had a great prayer life, but there are different kinds of prayer. Individual prayer is just you and God, and it is wonderful. There is also united, corporate prayer. It is another tremendous blessing. Repeatedly the Book of Acts says, *they* lifted up *their* voice with one accord. That is corporate prayer.

POWER IN CORPORATE PRAYER

Notice prayer makes tremendous power available to believers:

"The earnest (heartfelt, continued) prayer of a righteous man makes tremendous power available (dynamic in its working)." James 5:16, AMP

Peter had been thrown into prison but prayer "was made without ceasing of the church unto God for him" (Acts 12:5). Those people did not let discouragement take hold of them. They were not whining and complaining about Peter's dilemma. Instead, they started praying. As they were praying, the Lord sent an angel who appeared to Peter and set him free. Consequently, Peter immediately proceeded to the house where the prayer meeting was being held. Peter knew that he had been divinely delivered, and he knew it was because the church had been praying. What's more, he knew *where* they were praying.

"And when he had considered the thing, he came to the house of Mary the mother of John, whose surname was Mark; where many were gathered together praying."

Acts 12:12

How many were praying? *Many.* Now, it is good to pray by yourself. You can be very blessed that way. On the other hand, there is something very special when believers get together and the corporate anointing is flowing in prayer. There is a blessing there you cannot get any other way. It is true that you need to pray by yourself, but you also need to pray with other believers of "like" precious faith. The Bible says if one can put a thousand to flight, two can put ten thousand to flight (Deuteronomy 32:30).

The New Testament shows us examples of people praying by themselves. We see two of those when Peter went up on the housetop to pray alone, and when Jesus went up into the mountains to pray by himself. Many times, we also see a company of believers coming together to pray. A great company was praying for Peter that night. It was their prayers that prayed heaven's power down to set him free.

Paul and Barnabas were in the middle of that tremendous prayer victory. They saw the results of corporate prayer. They saw what took place in Jerusalem. They witnessed the plan of God being supernaturally prayed out. I imagine that they could not wait to get back to Antioch and share their experiences in prayer.

ADDING PRAYER AT ANTIOCH

The Bible says in Acts 13:1 that one of the very first things Paul and Barnabas did when they got back to Antioch was called a prayer meeting. They knew they had city-wide evangelism working. They also knew the saints had been taught well. Now, it was time to get everyone praying and spending time ministering to the Lord. Again, I am not saying Paul and Barnabas had never prayed before. I'm sure they did pray. From these verses, we can clearly see that something in them had changed after their return. They "caught" something, and it was very good. They caught the spirit of prayer.

ACTS 13 MEETINGS

Your private time with the Lord is so important. Praying by yourself is very beneficial, but corporate prayer adds another dimension to our communication with God. It was a very important part of early church life.

In Acts 4:23,31 the Bible says believers "lifted up their voice to God with one accord... And when they had prayed, the place was shaken where they were assembled; and they were all filled with the Holy Ghost, and they spoke the Word of God with boldness."

Notice they were all *together* praying and the Holy Ghost actually shook the building where they were assembled. We need some more prayer meetings like that. Notice they were all filled with the Holy Ghost again. We see that they were initially filled in Acts 2 and began speaking with other tongues. So, what happened here? They must have received fresh oil from heaven. They must have received fresh strength and a new charge from the Holy Ghost.

For several years, Cindy and I led prayer meetings like that all over Europe. We called them "Acts 13 Meetings." We traveled to different countries and invited pastors and ministers to come jointly to seek the Lord. We would spend two days ministering to the Lord and praying together. We may not have known what each pastor needed to do to solve their problems, but thank God the Holy Ghost did! As we spent time together in prayer, we laid a foundation in the spirit realm for God to move.

Several of the pastors testified that as we spent time in prayer, the Lord took care of a problem that they had been trying to solve for months. What happened? The Holy Ghost took hold together with them against those problems and answers came supernaturally. God provided and everyone rejoiced! Hallelujah!

Learn To Follow His Leading

In our "Acts 13 Meetings" we did not come to prayer with a specific agenda. Many times, we began to minister to the Lord and see what He would lead us to pray about. You know, Jesus is the head of the church and the Holy Spirit is the helper. We learned to collaborate and trust Him in those times of prayer. You can do the same. He wants to lead you in your prayer life. You can trust Him to give you utterance in the Holy Ghost. This is where prayer becomes a supernatural tool from God to help you out.

Many of the things I am doing in ministry today came out of times of prayer. I have had a lot of great ideas, but I could never talk the Lord into any of them. The ideas that always work best are those inspired by the Holy Ghost. Many times, they came while I was praying in other tongues.

Before we go preach in a nation, Cindy and I often begin to pick up that country in prayer. Sometimes we begin to pray out the name of a country, and other times the name of a city. Then there are times when we just seem to be burdened for a particular nation. Often, the Lord wanted to use us to pray for that nation and not go on a ministry trip. Above all, we do our best to follow the inward umpire and the peace of God in our hearts to get direction for our next endeavor.

Get Ahead in Prayer

I can always tell when I have not been praying enough. I struggle more with making decisions and knowing which way to go. Things just don't go smoothly. The favor I am used to walking in begins to wane. It is almost like I am falling behind in prayer. Now, if it is possible to be behind in prayer, then it is also possible to catch up and even "get ahead" in prayer.

We were so thankful to have a wonderful group of praying believers that the Lord put together to help our ministry. Our staff and prayer volunteers prayed together regularly. When Cindy and I were home we always tried to lead prayer time. What a difference it made for us when we were on the road ministering in different churches. Our prayer teams have paved the way for God to move in our services. It was evident that more spectacular things happened when we began to pray on a more regular basis.

Let me encourage you to take time to pray today and see if things go differently. The only way you will ever understand this is to experience it for yourself. You will become much more sensitive to God's voice. Favor and supernatural blessings will happen more often. I believe you will find yourself with a heart full of thanksgiving for His wonderful gift of praying in the Holy Ghost.

Chapter Nine
Following Your Inward Umpire

"Let the peace of God rule in your hearts, to the which
also ye are called in one body; and be ye thankful."
Colossians 3:15

Did you know that you are not the only one living on the inside of you? When a person is born again, the Holy Spirit comes to live in their heart (John 14:17). Now, as a child of God, that individual has the inward leading of the Holy Spirit to direct and guide them. What a gift has been given to mankind from our Father God! Now, it is up to us to learn to listen and follow our inward umpire called the Holy Ghost.

One of the greatest lessons that I ever learned is that we all have an umpire living on the inside of us. Notice Paul said to let God's peace rule in your hearts. The word "rule" is where we get our word for umpire. The Greek word is *brabevo*. The *Vines Expository Dictionary of New Testament Words* defines it like this: to act as an umpire, hence, generally, to arbitrate, to decide. The word "rule" in Colossians 3:15 means to arbitrate, representing the peace of Christ as deciding all matters in the heart of believers (revised version). Some regard the meaning as that of simple direction, control, or rule.

What does an umpire do? He makes decisions. Think of it the

same way we play baseball. If a runner comes sliding into home plate under the outstretched hands of the catcher, what do we wait for the umpire to do? The umpire will either put both arms out to the side and call the runner *safe*, or put his thumb up in the air and call the runner *out*. That is exactly what the peace of God does in your heart. It lets you know whether the decision you are about to make is "safe" or needs to be thrown "out."

If you don't have peace about a decision you are about to make, you need to throw it out, or at least slow down and pray about it some more. Sometimes it is not a wrong decision, just the wrong timing.

I like to explain it like this. Let's say you are driving along in your car approaching an intersection when the signal turns red. What do you do? You stop. If you don't, trouble and destruction will come into your life. If the light is green, you know it is okay to keep going.

Some lights are called caution lights. Most of them are flashing yellow lights which tell you to slow down and proceed *with caution*. It is an indication to pay extra attention. It might not be a good time to go through the intersection, so slow down a little. You may even stop for a while until you know it's safe to go on. That's what I mean by wrong timing.

There have been many times in my life that I had a part of the plan but there were things I was not seeing as clearly as I should. God sees everything, but very often we don't see the whole picture. By praying in the Holy Ghost, my directions became clearer. Knowing the best route to take saved me time, and money, and kept me from making any wrong turns.

> *"For my thoughts are not your thoughts,*
> *neither are your ways my ways, saith*
> *the Lord. For as the heavens are higher*
> *than the earth, so are my ways higher*
> *than your ways, and my thoughts than*
> *your thoughts... For ye shall go out with*
> *joy, and be led forth with peace."*
>
> *Isaiah 55:8-9,12*

This is another scripture that says God leads us with peace. His ways are higher than ours and His thoughts are higher than our thoughts. That is why you cannot make decisions the way the world does. The believer should not make choices based on what you can see or with just natural facts. God gave us our minds. We use them to help us evaluate the decisions we should make. In any case, always remember to check in with your umpire. The Holy Ghost may know some things you don't. There may be something about to happen that your mind does not see coming, but He does.

BE CAREFUL LISTENING FOR VOICES

It's good to learn to follow God's peace in your heart. When God speaks to you, it is not necessarily with His voice. Most of the time He leads us by that inward umpire. That is His inward peace in your heart.

Be careful seeking for voices. The Bible says in 1 Corinthians 14:10, *"There are, it may be, so many kinds of voices in the world, and none of them is without signification."* All voices come from somewhere, but not all voices are God's voice. Most of us have found that out the hard way. Sometimes a person may think they have heard the Lord tell them something, but later realize it was not God's voice that they heard.

That is why I am extra careful about following voices. I always check everything by two golden rules.

First of all, is it scriptural? Does it line up with God's Word? God will never tell you to do something that opposes His Word.

For instance, God will never tell you to marry someone else's spouse. Why? Because God's Word says to not covet another man's spouse. I've heard people say, "The Holy Spirit told me to do this." It may have been some spirit, but it was not the Holy Spirit. First John 5:6-8 says, that the Word and the Spirit always agree. Check to make sure that whatever voice you are listening to agrees with God's Word.

What Does It Mean To Bear Witness?

Secondly, I check every voice to make sure it bears witness to my spirit. Romans 8:14-16 says:

> *"For as many as are led by the Spirit of*
> *God, they are the sons of God. The Spirit*
> *itself beareth witness with our spirit,*
> *that we are the children of God."*

If someone asks you, "How do you know you are saved? How do you know you're going to heaven when you die?" What will your answer be? You should answer something like this, "I'm saved because the Word says I am." When you believe in your heart that God raised Jesus from the dead and confess with your mouth that Jesus is Lord, you shall be saved. Not you *might* be saved. You *shall* be! (Romans 10:9-10)

> *"These things have I written unto you that*
> *Believe on the name of the Son of God; that*
> *ye may know that ye have eternal life."*
> *1 John 5:13*

Notice this does not mean that you will receive eternal life someday. Eternal life does not begin when you die; eternal life begins the moment you make Jesus the Lord of your life. The very second you get saved, God's life and nature move on the inside of your heart. You are now born again and your eternal life with Jesus has started right then.

In my church, we thought you had to wait until you died to see if you went up or down. Everything was based on our work. If we had done enough and were good enough to pass God's test, we went to heaven. If we were not good enough, we went to hell. The problem is that you just *hoped* you were good enough, and always had a horrible feeling that you never could measure up. The truth of the matter is that every one of us must come to God based on what He did for us. We have to receive the free gift of salvation purchased by the blood of Jesus, not by our own works. You can know right now that you are saved and going to heaven. This is the first step to following God's plan for your life. Give your heart to Jesus Christ and receive His free gift.

Not Based on Feelings

The second reason you know you are saved is because something way down on the inside of you knows you are going to heaven. That is the Holy Ghost bearing witness with your spirit.

Notice that the Holy Spirit does not bear witness to our feelings. Nowhere in the Bible will you find any verse that says God bears witness to our feelings. Our feelings can be up one day and down the next, but we do not have to be ruled by them. Someday you may wake up and not "feel" saved. The devil will help you out. He will tell you that you are not saved. He will tell you Christianity is crazy, and that God does not even exist. When that happens, just get this scripture out and begin to quote it:

"For God so loved the world, that he gave His only begotten Son, that whosoever believeth in him should not perish, but have everlasting life."

John 3:16

As you do, suddenly the peace of God will flood back into your heart. That's because the Holy Ghost in your heart always agrees with the Word of God. If you are having doubts about any part of God's Word, find scriptures that promise what you need. Begin to meditate on those scriptures and then confess them out loud. Peace will begin to reign in your heart once more.

Are you having trouble believing in God for your healing? Begin to meditate on God's healing promises. The Holy Ghost who lives in your heart will bear witness with those scriptures and true faith will rise on the inside of you.

Now, here's the greatest part: This same principle can be followed in every area of your life. Are you struggling with direction, or what to do in life? The Holy Ghost will also bear witness with your spirit about which way you should go.

You are not going to find a scripture that tells you exactly who to marry, which car to buy, which house to live in, or which job to take. However, the Holy Ghost does want to lead you. He does that by the inward witness. Listen to your inward umpire and follow after peace in your heart.

Don't Be Pressured by the Devil

When Cindy and I first began to travel in ministry on our own, a certain pastor of a large church invited us to come minister for him. He said if we were ever going to be in the area, to just call him and he would schedule some meetings.

I started planning a trip to his part of the country. One day I began to call his church to talk to him. After I dialed the phone number, I felt very uneasy and I hung up. I thought to myself, *"Oh, I will just call him later."*

The next day, the same thing happened again. I dialed his number and then hung up when I heard it ring on the other end. This time I decided to write him a letter. I was about to give it to my secretary to mail, but for some reason, it just did not seem right. I decided to just let that letter sit on my desk for a while and it did for several days.

The next week, as I sat working in my office, the devil came to help me plan my schedule. Have you ever had the devil try to "help" you plan your life? The devil always works by applying pressure. He always tries to force you into making a decision. If you are feeling pressured, put on the brakes.

God never forces people to do anything. God *leads* by His Spirit. Colossians says He leads us with peace. We follow Him by following after that peace. Most of the time the decisions we make under pressure do not have to be made right then anyway. If we step back away from the decision for a moment, regroup, and pray a little bit, things will become so much clearer. God's wisdom will begin to flow. We can then make a plan led by our spirit, not something the devil pressured us into doing.

That day the devil began to pressure me by saying things like, "You better call that pastor. You know he has a big church and his schedule is going to get full if you don't call him." The devil began to antagonize me: "What are you going to do about that?" Then it got a little louder and faster. "What are you going to do about that? What are you going to do about that?"

Finally, I just yelled out in my office, "All right! All right! I'll call him." I got his phone number out and began to dial. It started ringing on the other end. Then, it happened again. I just could not do it. I knew on the inside that something was off so I slammed the phone down.

Can you see that my umpire was trying to tell me something? I did not have peace; I had pressure. Every time I tried to call, something on the inside of me didn't seem quite right. That was the inward witness of the Holy Spirit trying to get my attention.

Why wouldn't God let us go to that church?

We found out later that this pastor had started to get away from the Word of God. He began to teach things that did not line up with the counsel of God's Word. God did not want us in the middle of that. He did not want us putting our stamp of approval on what that pastor was doing. Even more, God did not want us to waste our time. Sadly, I don't even think that church is in existence today. That is what happens when you get away from the Word of God.

In the Book of Acts, God sent the evangelist Phillip to Samaria where they had a city-wide crusade. Do you know where God sent the now famous evangelist Phillip next? God sent him to the back side of the desert for one Ethiopian man. God knew exactly what He was doing. Phillip went to minister to that *one* man, but history tells us the story. That one Ethiopian man went back to his country and through him, Christianity spread around the whole region. God is so smart!

Do you know where God sent us? We went to a church that

was just starting. We had a wonderful time there! God moved and they have ended up being lifelong friends. That new little church began to grow, thrive, and became a blessing to that whole area. We would have missed it if I had followed my natural thinking, caved into the pressure, and gone to that other church. Jesus knows right where we need to be to help build His Kingdom.

Not My Will, But Thine Be Done

One time Cindy and I got invited to go overseas with a friend of ours. The timing of the trip could not have been worse for us. It was right in the middle of the only time we had scheduled to be home. We had been on the road for over two months at that time, and we were looking forward to being at our home for a week.

I know I haven't learned everything in all my years of marriage, but one thing is certain, it is not good to add a trip instead of staying home for some much-needed time off. I jokingly say, "That is going where angels fear to tread." Cindy loves to travel, but she also enjoys waking up in her own bed every now and then. We had another overseas trip planned just two months later. Financially it would have been difficult for us to take two trips in that short amount of time. We decided we just could not go.

A week later, we were ministering at a church in another state. I was praying about what to preach that night, but all I could think about was the overseas ministry trip we had turned down. I was trying to get direction for that night's service, but all I kept hearing in my spirit was the name of that country. I kept saying, "Lord, I don't want to talk about that right now. We already said we could not go." That did not stop the Lord.

After this went on for three or four days, the Lord finally got it over to me that He wanted us to go on that trip.

I did not hear an audible voice that said, "Thou must go!" I did not have an angel appear to me. Every time I thought about going on the trip, it just seemed right.

I could not get away from it in prayer. Every time I thought about the decision we had made not to go, I had an uneasy feeling in my spirit. It made me not want to pray or read my Bible. That's because I was going against that inward umpire. My spirit was telling me I had made the wrong decision.

I made a deal with the Lord. I said, "Lord, we will go on one condition: You have to tell my wife that we are supposed to go." I have learned a few things in my years of marriage. Cindy hears the voice of the Spirit just like I do, and I needed Him to talk to her.

After a few days passed, I tried to figure out how to ask Cindy if she had heard anything from the Lord. I kind of hinted around and then finally just asked, "Have you thought any more about going on that mission trip we said we could not go on?"

She looked up and said with a far-off look, "Well…" I could tell from the sound of her voice that the Lord had been talking to her, too. Then she said, "Maybe the Lord does want us to go." On the outside, I acted like Mr. Cool, but on the inside, I was doing Holy Ghost flips! I knew we had heard from God and that He was going to do something very special.

It is wonderful to follow your umpire. The Holy Ghost always knows where you need to be. Incredible signs and wonders happened on that trip. We met up with another former member of the Rhema Singers & Band, as well as an evangelist friend named Rudy. In those meetings, the Holy Ghost began to flow and demonstrate Himself through psalms, hymns, and spiritual songs. The glory of God filled the services every night. The pastor of the church was excited. He testified that the Holy Ghost made deposits into his musicians when they saw how the Spirit of God flowed through all of us.

Sometimes it helps to see other people flow in the Holy Ghost. It helps us to know what to do when we sense that same anointing begins to move in our services.

One night the glory of God came into the service in a mighty way. Rudy took off dancing in the Holy Ghost and then my wife began to get the Holy Ghost giggles. Holy Ghost joy hit that church. I am sure they had never seen or experienced anything like that before. To make a long story short, the Lord miraculously changed many people's lives that night.

One lady in the service had polio. She needed braces and crutches to pull herself along. She was completely healed that night! It was one of the most amazing miracles we had ever seen. She was so grateful to the Lord. She *walked* up the ten steps to the church platform and brought her offering to the Lord. Everyone rejoiced at the awesome miracle that God had done for her. At the end of the service, we tried to give her back the braces and crutches. She said, "I don't need those things anymore!" She threw them down and marched victoriously out the back of the church. She was praising God as she went.

I'm so glad we followed our umpire. In the natural, it looked like there was no way that we could go. Something down on the inside kept leading us to step out in faith and obey God.

By the time we got home, we had every penny we needed to not only pay not only for our trip but also enough money to run our ministry while we were gone. That was another miracle! God is so good!

What God leads you to do He will provide for... if you will trust Him. What you think up, you get to pay for. If you ever have a few of those projects that you pay for, you will learn in a hurry to follow the leading of the Holy Spirit.

EXTRA GOOD NEWS!

It is an adventure learning to follow the inward umpire. He will lead you to success and victory in every single endeavor. He knows your future better than you do. If we would just learn to follow that inward peace, God would be able to help us in every area of our lives. We would make better job and business decisions. We would make better decisions with our money, our relationships, and with our families. There is not a single area of your life that God is not concerned about. He wants to help with every decision that emerges in life. The choice is ours. He has made Himself available to assist us. We just need to follow after peace and trust in His ability to help us.

Jesus said perilous times would come, so don't let your heart be troubled. He was sending the Comforter, our Helper, the Holy Spirit to live on the inside of us to lead us. We would have an advantage over the enemy when the Holy Spirit came to live on the inside of His children.

Jesus said in John 14:18: *"I will not leave you comfortless"* (KJV). We are so thankful for that. The original Greek translation says, "I will not leave you as an orphan." The definition of an orphan is a child born into this world who is deprived by death, of one or usually both parents.

It also indicates one who is deprived of protection or advantage. God did not bring you into this wonderful new life through the new birth to leave you alone–orphaned. He does not expect you to grow up spiritually all by yourself. Thank God, we have a helper. He is our umpire. He is the Holy Spirit living on the inside of us to help reign in life.

MENTAL ENERGY VS. HOLY GHOST DIRECTION

Over the years, I have had a lot of good ideas to help the Lord with our ministry. I would see a need and devise a wonderful plan to help the Lord out. The only problem is, I could never talk to the Lord into any of my great ideas! He wanted Cindy and me to do something else with the time, talents, and ministry He had given us. I have had a lot of good ideas that I have asked the Lord to bless. I finally discovered it is best to find out what the Lord's plan is and do that. After all, His plan is already blessed!

I call all the good ideas I came up with "mental energy." Our minds are a wonderful tool given to us by God. God certainly gave us our minds to use and to create, but not to lead us. The Holy Spirit through our spirit has been sent to lead and guide us.

Mental energy can be driven by worry. It will cost you time and it will make you tired.

You are a three-part being. You are a spirit. You have a soul, and you live in a body (1 Thessalonians 5:23). Each part of you has a voice. We are familiar with the voice of our mind and our body, but our spirit also has a voice. We call it the still small voice, or the inward witness. Most of the time by following your spirit you will not actually hear an audible voice, but rather sense an inward witness of peace.

> *"Let the peace of God rule in your*
> *hearts, to the which also ye are called in*
> *one body; and be ye thankful."*
> *Colossians 3:15*

The Worrell translation of the New Testament says, "Let the peace of God be your umpire," and that is exactly what the original Greek says. We need to learn to follow that inward umpire. If we would, our lives would be filled with success after success.

Many times we battle with decisions in our minds. We try to figure out which way to go based on our own mental knowledge. Your friends will also lend you their mental energy and try to help you make decisions. Is that the Lord's way? No. I have found that when I spend a little extra time praying about my decisions, my direction becomes clearer. Learn to pray out the plan of God for your life. Things I have prayed out ahead of time have always been the most successful–not only in our ministry but in our personal lives as well.

As we grow in our Christian walk, we will learn to distinguish the difference between the Holy Ghost and our own "mental energy."

Sometimes in business meetings, I like to get quiet while everyone else is talking and just check in with my umpire. Often, I am not even conscious of His leading until later. I then realized it was when I got quiet that I saw exactly what we needed to do. Learn to listen to your heart. That umpire on the inside of you is full of wisdom and certainly knows more about the future than you do.

I have found over the years that it is when my mind gets quiet that the Holy Ghost can speak to me and get my attention. As long as our minds are constantly busy and filled with other things, we will not learn to follow our spirit. It is good to become more aware of your spirit man and the Holy Spirit living in you. This is being "spirit conscious."

We need to learn to stay balanced on this. It seems it is the hardest thing for the body of Christ to go down the middle of the road. They go from one ditch to the other. Yes, it is good to use our minds. God has given us our minds to make decisions. He has given us common sense. We do not need to pray about whether we should brush our teeth today or not. We need to use our minds to make sensible decisions in life.

The Lord is also endeavoring to give out new ideas and witty inventions in the last days to bless His children. He wants to give us creative thoughts and ideas that are different from the way that everyone else is doing things, but we need to know how to follow that umpire on the inside of us.

Don't Be Overly Cautious

Have you ever been driving and noticed an overly cautious driver? They're the ones who drive so slowly that they become a traffic hazard to others. That is the way some people are with being led by the Holy Spirit and making decisions in life. They are so afraid that they are going to miss God's will, therefore they never make any decisions. Fear paralyzes them and they do not enjoy life.

Did you ever notice while driving a car, we are less aware of the green lights than the red ones? You can keep driving and keep going forward as long as the lights stay green. The moment one turns red, it gets your attention and you come to a stop.

That is the way I am in life as well. I just keep going ahead following after peace and the desire of my heart. I know the moment something is wrong. I get a yellow caution light or a red stop light. Then my inward umpire goes off. Sometimes with me, it seems just like a buzzer.

I know Bible school graduates who have been sitting idle for years waiting for direction from the Lord. Many say direction has never come. I have often wondered if those folks are just too afraid to miss it, so they have never done anything. Many of them grow cold and some end up backsliding. Sure, we do not want to miss the leading of the Lord, but God knows that. Even if we do step out and miss it, God is well able to guide us back to the right place.

You may be struggling with this issue right now. Maybe you think you have missed God so many times that there is no way for you to ever get back on track. That just is not so! You must choose to believe that God loves you so much that He would move heaven and earth to find you. He will help you get on the right path.

Isn't that just like a loving heavenly Father? He cares about you and what you are going through. He wants you to be a success. He wants you to do what's right just as much as you do... maybe even more! He's given you His Word to teach you. You have the Holy Spirit to lead and guide you. The Name of Jesus also belongs to you, so that you can conquer all things. I encourage you to rise up and follow God's plan for your life.

My dad taught me a valuable lesson when I was learning to drive a car. It is much easier to turn a moving car than one that's parked. It is also much easier for God to lead you in life if you are moving or at least attempting to do something. Just step out in faith, trust your heart, and enjoy life as you go.

The Apostle Paul even had an experience like this. He received a commission from the Lord to take the Gospel to the Gentile nations of the world. In Acts 16, Paul had spent quite a while preaching and establishing churches throughout Galatia, but now he sensed it was time for him to move on.

They tried to go to Asia, but the Bible says they were forbidden by the Holy Ghost to preach the Word in Asia. Later, Paul went to Asia and established a Bible school there. The Bible says all of Asia heard the Word of God because of the graduates of that school. God knows when an area is ready to hear the Gospel.

Then they tried to go to Bithynia, but the Spirit suffered them not to go there either. The Bible does not say how the Spirit forbade them, but I believe it was the same way God leads us all: by that inward witness.

Then Paul received a vision from the Lord to go preach in Macedonia, or what is now part of present-day Europe. We may not always have such spectacular leadings as dreams or visions, but your direction will come as a leading of inward peace. Notice Paul did not get any direction until he stepped out to go somewhere. He tried to go to two different places and each time the Holy Ghost said "no," but then direction came as he stepped out to go.

Many times, if I am not sure something is the Lord's will, I will take a step in that direction. I don't always know if something is right until I take that first step. The moment I do, I get clearer insight. I know more as I go. Then if it is the wrong way, I will know it because… there is no peace following it.

GOD GIVES US THE DESIRES OF OUR HEARTS

Fear of failure has robbed so many of their God-given dreams and visions. It has deprived them of new plans and desires to have a better life and things. It is a thief. God wants to give you the desires of your heart. Learn to trust your heart and follow His leading.

> *"Delight thyself also in the Lord and He shall give thee the desires of thine heart"*
>
> *(Psalms 37:4).*

I had an instructor in Bible school who loved this verse. Most people think this verse means that God will give us the things we want or desire. This teacher had a little different slant on it. He said as we delight in the Lord to do His will, God will make His desires, our desires. I really believe that. As we walk in fellowship with God, endeavoring to be obedient to Him, His desires become our desires and we actually want to do the will of God. When you are consistently living that kind of life, you can trust the desires of your heart.

You do not want to follow the desires of your flesh, your mind, or of the devil. That is where the Word comes in. The Word of God has been given to teach you not to follow the lust of the flesh. As long as you are not contradicting God's Word, or doing something God's Word says not to do, you can follow the desires of your heart. You can trust the instincts of your heart.

God places in you the desire to do His will. The key is delighting yourself in the Lord and walking in fellowship with Him.

"For it is God which worketh in you both to will and to do of his good pleasure."

Philippians 2:13

Here are some other translations of that verse:

"(Not in your own strength) for it is God
Who is all the while effectually at work
In you (energizing and creating in you the power
and desire), both to will and to work for His good
pleasure and satisfaction and delight."
Philippians 2:13, Amplified

"God is always at work in you to make you
willing and able to obey his own purpose."
Philippians 2:13, Good News

"God is the One who is constantly putting forth His
energy in you, both in the form of your being desirous of

and our doing His good pleasure."

Philippians 2:13, Wuest

"It is God Himself whose power creates within you the desire to do His gracious will and also brings about the accomplishment of the desire."

Philippians 2:13, Weymouth

"It is God who is all the while supplying the impulse, giving you the power to resolve, the strength to perform, the execution of His good pleasure."

Philippians 2:13, Way

As you spend time praying in the Holy Ghost, you are giving the Holy Spirit time to mold His desires into your heart. You are giving the Holy Spirit time to speak to you and guide you.

Most of the time in my ministry I have been led to do what I enjoyed. I follow the desire I have to do something, believing God placed that desire there. Sometimes I get the feeling that we think God is going to make us do things we do not want to do. Not so. Even if He calls you to be a missionary in some remote country, you will be happy. God will give you the desire within to be there. You will want to do it.

If you are doing something you know He told you to do and are not happy, ask Him to help you. Ask Him where you need to make an adjustment. God wants you to be happy and enjoy life. He can help you find joy, peace, and success in any situation.

Learn to enjoy life with Christ. Follow the desires of your heart. As you delight yourself in Him, you will walk from victory to victory. You can fulfill God's plan for your life!

Chapter Ten
Staying Balanced

I have shared the importance of praying in tongues. I also want to give you one more piece of the puzzle, so to speak, on the subject of prayer.

"What is it then, I will pray with the spirit, and I will pray with the understanding also. I will sing with the spirit and I will sing with the understanding also."
1 Corinthians 14:15

We see in this passage that Paul prayed two ways. He prayed with the Spirit, but he also prayed with the *understanding.*

Don't just pray in other tongues all the time. You need to pray both with tongues and your understanding. If all you ever do is pray in other tongues, you will get off or become flaky. I have seen people like that, haven't you? They pray all day long in other tongues, and never with their understanding. They get off spiritually. It is good to pray in other tongues, and you should do that a lot. Where is the balance? You need to read your Bible and pray with your understanding as well.

What does that mean? It means you need to pray in your native language. You need to have a relationship with God with your understanding. Why is that so important? Jesus talked about that.

> *"If you abide in me and my words abide in you, then you will ask what you will and it shall be done unto you."*

John 15:7

God's Word has an important part to play in your prayer life. The more of God's Word you have in your heart, the more solid your foundation is concerning what you are believing God for.

For instance, if you need healing, find good scriptures that cover healing. Claim them. Quote them. Write them down and put them on the refrigerator or the bathroom mirror. Confess those scriptures and tell yourself that you are what God says you are. Remind yourself (and God) that He took your infirmities and bore your sicknesses. See yourself healed by His stripes.

> *"Who his own self bare our sins in his own body on the tree, that we, being dead to sins, should live unto righteousness: by whose stripes ye were healed."*

1 Peter 2:24

Remind God of His Word. As you do, you will be expressing yourself to God and building faith in your heart. Guess what? That is prayer, too! Your prayer life needs to be filled with the Word of God. The Word will give you a solid foundation for faith and make you stable.

Pray both ways! They are most effective together. As you pray in part with your understanding and in part with the Holy Ghost in other tongues, your prayer life blossoms and becomes effective.

A LIFESTYLE, NOT JUST A FEELING

I first got filled with the Holy Ghost during the Charismatic Revival in the 1970s. I got so excited about God that I prayed in the Spirit every day. After a couple of years that excitement began to wear off. It is like a child who pesters his parents for a new toy. It is something that he absolutely must have! After he gets it, he plays with it every day for about two weeks. Shortly the newness wears off, and he's onto something else.

Sometimes, if we are not careful with the things of God, we will treat them just like that child with a new toy. It is exciting! It is fresh and wonderful, but when the "new" wears off, we quickly move on to something else.

I noticed after I had been filled with the Holy Ghost for a couple of years that I was not praying with the enthusiasm I used to. God gently started dealing with me about that. He said, "When you first got filled with the Holy Ghost, it was new and exciting. Now, tell me, Bruce, what causes you to act on the Word?"

"Faith," I replied, "and faith comes by hearing and hearing by the Word."

Then the Lord said, "Bruce, the only way you are going to act on My Word is to get a hold of the revelation of what you are doing when you pray in the Spirit. If you get into the Word on the subject, you will see all the blessings and benefits of praying in the Holy Ghost and spending time with me. Faith will arise in your heart to do it. You will not be driven by emotion but by faith. You will be so excited about all the benefits that whether you feel like it or not, you will give yourself to prayer. Revelation and light from the Word will help you to develop prayer as a lifestyle and not just a feeling."

The truths I have shown you from the Word of God have been designed to give you a foundation for a consistent prayer life. Start with five minutes a day. You will enjoy talking and being with the Lord so much that five minutes just will not be enough. You will move to ten minutes, and then ten minutes won't satisfy you. Before too long, you will find yourself *looking* for ways to spend time with God.

A friend of mine pointed out a truth that really blessed me. They showed me that if we prayed in the Holy Ghost for 15 minutes every day, at the end of one year we would have prayed over 90 hours of the perfect will of God for our lives. Wow! Isn't that great? Anyone can find 15 minutes a day for prayer. Maybe pray for five minutes while you are in the shower and five minutes while you are driving to work. Maybe five more minutes while doing something else. Can you imagine the difference it would make to pray 90 hours of the perfect will of God for your life this year?

Don't let another day go by without tapping into the amazing tool God has made available to help you in life. Pray in the Spirit!

Chapter Eleven
You Can Pray in the Holy Ghost

I realize some of you reading this book may not be filled with the Holy Ghost. You may not know how to pray in other tongues… But you can! It is not only a good idea, it is a tremendous blessing that belongs to every believer. Jesus commanded His disciples to be filled with the Holy Ghost.

> *"And, being assembled with them, He commanded them that they should not depart from Jerusalem, but wait for the promise of the Father, which He said, 'You have heard of me. For John truly baptized with water, but you shall be baptized with the Holy Ghost not many days hence… You shall receive power after that the Holy Ghost is come upon you: and you shall be witnesses unto me.'"*

Acts 1: 4-5,8

That power is not only to bless you and strengthen you to be a better Christian but also so that God's supernatural power can flow through you to bless others.

That is why I wanted to be filled with the Holy Ghost. God made a way for His power to better flow through us to bless others who need it. That same power turned a cowardly Peter and the rest of Jesus' disciples into mighty men of courage with boldness. They had supernatural signs and miracles following their lives. Why? Because they were filled with the Holy Ghost and power. He did the same for me! He filled me with boldness! The good news is that it is for everyone.

ANYONE CAN RECEIVE

"For I say unto you, ask, and it shall be given you; seek, and ye shall find; knock, and it shall be opened unto you. For every one that asketh receiveth; and he that seeketh findeth; and to him that knocketh it shall be opened. If a son knocketh it shall be opened. If a son shall ask bread of any of you that is a father, will he give him a stone? Or if he asks a fish, will he for a fish give him a serpent? Or if he shall ask an egg, will he offer him a scorpion? If ye then, being evil, know how to give good gifts unto your children; how much more shall your heavenly Father give the Holy Spirit to them that ask him?"

Luke 11:9-13

Jesus said in this portion of scripture that everyone who asks for the gift of the Holy Spirit can receive. Who does that include? If Jesus said everyone, He meant *everyone.*

What's going to happen to people when they get filled? The same thing happened to believers on the day of Pentecost. The Holy Spirit has never, ever changed. We receive the same Holy Spirit they did in the Bible. If we find out what happened to these men and women, then we can know what to expect when we are filled.

THE BIBLICAL EXAMPLE

*"And when the day of Pentecost was fully come, they
were all with one accord in one place. And suddenly
there came a sound from heaven as of a rushing mighty
wind, and it filled all the house where they were sitting.
And there appeared unto them cloven tongues like as
of fire, and it sat upon each of them. And they were all
filled with the Holy Ghost, and began to speak with
other tongues, as the Spirit gave them utterance."*

Acts 2:1-4

Notice they were *all* filled, and then they *all* began to speak
with other tongues.

Someone might ask, "Do I have to speak in tongues to be filled
with the Holy Spirit?" I always respond by saying, "No, but you
get to!" Tongues come along with the infilling of the Holy Spirit.
Similarly, when you buy a new pair of tennis shoes, the tongue
just comes along with the shoe. It is the same when you are filled
with the Holy Spirit. Speaking in other tongues just comes along
with the package. It is a wonderful benefit of being filled.

HAVE YOU RECEIVED SINCE YOU BELIEVED?

*1 And it came to pass, that, while Apollos was at
Corinth, Paul having passed through the upper coasts
came to Ephesus: and finding certain disciples,
2 He said unto them, Have ye received the Holy Ghost
since ye believed? And they said unto him, We have not
so much as heard whether there be any Holy Ghost.
3 And he said unto them, Unto what then were ye
baptized? And they said, Unto John's baptism.
4 Then said Paul, John verily baptized with the
baptism of repentance, saying unto the people, that
they should believe on him which should come after*

him, that is, on Christ Jesus.
5 When they heard this, they were baptized in the
name of the Lord Jesus.
6 And when Paul had laid his hands upon them,
the Holy Ghost came on them, and they spake with
tongues, and prophesied.

Acts 19:1-6

We see that Paul went to Ephesus and found certain *disciples*. I love what Paul asked them: "Have you received the Holy Ghost since you believed?" Notice, it was normal to receive the Holy Ghost *after* you believe or receive Jesus Christ. They responded by saying, "We have not even heard of the Holy Ghost." There are a lot of people like that today. You can't receive what you don't know.

The Bible says to go into all the world and preach the gospel (Mark 16:15). It also says that faith comes by hearing and hearing by the Word of God (Romans 10:17). They needed to hear about Jesus and the baptism of the Holy Ghost to be able to receive. Paul preached Christ to them, and they were baptized in His name. They could have stopped right there like many believers do, but they did not. Paul laid his hands on them and they were filled with the Holy Ghost and spoke with other tongues. Notice that tongues came along with receiving the Holy Ghost. The same thing will happen to you when you are filled with the Holy Spirit.

HAVE TONGUES CEASED?

"...but whether there be tongues, they shall cease; whether there be knowledge, it shall vanish away. For we know in part, and we prophesy in part. But when that which is perfect is come, then that which is in part shall be done away. For now, we see through a glass, darkly; but then face to face: now I know in part; but then shall I know even as also I am known." 1 Corinthians 13:8-12

Some denominations say that speaking in other tongues has passed away, or that speaking in tongues is not for today. They generally pull this scripture in I Corinthians 13:8 out of context to prove this untrue theory. It does say tongues shall cease, that much is true. However, if you read that verse in context with the whole chapter, you will find out it goes on to say *when* tongues shall cease.

Tongues will cease when we see God "face to face." When does that happen? When we get to heaven! When you get to heaven you will not need to pray in the Holy Ghost and build yourself up. There will not be any mysteries. There will not be any more tests or trials. You will have a glorified body. So, yes, *then* tongues will cease. As long as we are down here in this world, we can pray in the Holy Ghost and build ourselves up. Thank God! We can pray out divine secrets. The Holy Ghost will take hold together with us against our problems and help us pray.

RIGHTLY DIVIDING THE WORD

Are tongues for everyone or just some special people?

"While Peter yet spake these words, the Holy Ghost fell on all them which heard the word. And they of the circumcision which believed were astonished, as many as came with Peter, because that on the Gentiles also was poured out the gift of the Holy Ghost.
For they heard them speak with tongues, and magnify God."

Acts 10:44-47

How wonderful that salvation *and* the gift of the Holy Ghost are for everyone. As Peter was preaching about Jesus, the Holy Ghost was poured out not only on the Jews but on the Gentiles as well. Notice what happened when they received it. They began to speak with tongues and give God all the praise. The baptism of the Holy Spirit and speaking with tongues always go together.

Some people incorrectly teach that tongues are for some people today but not everyone. They pull this scripture out of context:

"Are all apostles? Are all prophets? Are all teachers? Are all workers of miracles? Have all the gifts of healing? Do all speak with tongues? Do all interpret?"

1 Corinthians 12:29-30

The answer to the question is obviously no. You must realize, however, just what Paul is talking about here. Notice these are all ministry gifts. He is not talking about believers being filled with the Holy Spirit and fellowshipping with God in their new heavenly language. He is not talking about the initial baptism of the Holy Ghost. He is talking about a special ministry gift of other tongues in operation.

Have you ever heard someone stand up in church and speak in tongues, and then they (or other people) interpret that in English or their native language? Well, that is an example of what Paul is talking about here. God is not going to use everyone that way, just like everyone is not going to be an apostle or a prophet. In the Bible, when believers were filled with the Holy Spirit, it clearly says they spoke with other tongues, or it implies they did.

Remember Jesus said that everyone who asks for the Holy Ghost would receive. If not, He would be unfair. We could accuse God of being unjust and a respecter of persons, willing to help only some in this way, but not all. No. Thank God, Jesus said everyone who asks shall receive. It is a gift just like salvation that is available to ALL who will receive it.

PAUL SPOKE WITH TONGUES

We have a record of the Apostle Paul being filled with the Holy Ghost in Acts chapter 10 when Ananias laid his hands on him. It does not say he spoke with other tongues right there, but we know he did. Later, Paul talked about it when writing to the Corinthian church.

"I thank my God, I speak with tongues more than ye all."

1 Corinthians 14:18

He said he prayed in the Holy Ghost more than the whole church put together. Not only that, he said, "I thank my God, I speak with tongues more than ye all." Why was he thankful? It must have been a great blessing to him.

You Do the Talking, Not the Holy Ghost

Notice again in Acts 2:4 that the people who gathered together were all filled with the Holy Ghost, and *they* all began to speak with other tongues as the Holy Spirit gave *them* the utterance. Some people think God is going to turn on a radio or start a YouTube episode down on the inside of them, and then a new language will start coming out. It is not like that at all. The Holy Ghost gave them the utterance (the new language), but **they** did the speaking.

You are not going to get a new voice. Everything you use to talk to me or anyone else, you will use to talk to the Lord in this new language. It will be your air, your voice, and your vocal cords. The only difference is that the Holy Spirit is going to come and fill you. He will give you a desire to speak out in a brand-new language you have never spoken before.

As you start, it may seem like baby talk. It may seem like some strange, and different language. As you receive, the Holy Spirit will give you a desire to speak that language out. It may begin as only one or two little syllables. Sometimes, when people get filled, they start speaking in a fluent language. Others, like me, only have one or two little words. As you pray in the Spirit and yield to the Holy Ghost, that language begins to grow.

Often people wait for the Holy Spirit to do everything. If I tried to talk to you but never opened my mouth to speak, how would you understand me? You would not. It is the same way with our heavenly language. You will have to open up your mouth and take a step of faith.

The moment you ask God to fill you, He will give you a desire to speak out in that brand-new language. It is easy to receive: Just repeat this prayer. Ask the Lord to fill you. It is His will.

> **Father, I come to You in the mighty Name of Jesus!**
> **I am asking You to fill me with Your precious Holy**
> **Spirit. I believe I will speak in tongues according to**
> **Acts 2:4. I can see that the baptism in the Holy Ghost**
> **is Your gift to me. Therefore, I release my faith and**
> **I fully expect to speak with other tongues, as the**
> **Spirit gives me utterance. Lord, I receive right now!**
> **Thank You for filling me!**

Now, take a big breath and yield to Him. Begin to worship Him in your new prayer language. Let His anointing and presence come and fill you until you are overflowing. Believe it and receive it right now!

AFTER YOU RECEIVE

The Bible declares the devil is a liar, and one of the first things he likes to tell people after they are filled is, "That's just you doing the talking. That's not the Holy Ghost." Well, sure it's you doing the talking. Who else is going to use your mouth, your air, and your lips? It is you, but it is the Holy Ghost *giving* you your new language. Throw caution to the wind and put doubt behind you. Do not listen to the devil.

You should pray in that new language every day. Remember Paul said in 1 Corinthians 14:18: *"I thank my God, I speak with tongues more than ye all."* He said that he prayed in tongues more than the whole church in Corinth put together because it blessed and benefited him.

You can pray in the Holy Ghost anytime you want to or need to.

> *"What is it then? I will pray with the Spirit, and I will pray with the understanding also: I will sing with the spirit, and I will sing with the understanding also."*
>
> ### 1 Corinthians 14:15

Who is doing the praying and the singing? Paul was in control of how he prayed and how he sang. It was his choice. He said, "I will pray with the spirit, and I will pray with the understanding of my known language." You can pray at will and you should. Anytime you need to build yourself up, or you don't know what to do, begin to pray in the Holy Ghost. Watch God supernaturally unfold His plan and will into your life.

Chapter Twelve
A Final Word

There is nothing like spending time with God in prayer. Your love for Him will always grow to new levels as you pray. God has created you and me to fellowship with Him. He wants to talk to you, and he wants you to talk to Him. He wants you to know Him. He wants to pour his love out on you. There is just something on the inside of every person that will never be satisfied in life until they have this type of communion with their heavenly Father.

This is the type of Christian life that becomes an adventure in God. You were created to walk with the One who gave you life. Realize there is more to life than just your everyday tasks. You can be like Jesus and be doing the Father's will. You can know Him and be doing kingdom business.

Get comfortable with the Holy Spirit, and allow Him to use you in prayer. Then as you allow Him to use you in prayer, your life will be full to overflowing with blessings. I believe the courses of churches, cities, and whole nations can be turned to the Lord as we allow God to use us in prayer, as the Holy Spirit gives us utterance. Yield to Him today. Realize the impact you can have by standing in the gap for your family, friends, and the work of God around the world.

"For I know the plans I have for you," declares the Lord, "plans to prosper you and not to harm you, plans to give you hope and a future. Then you will call on me and come and pray to me, and I will listen to you. You will seek me and find me when you seek me with all your heart."

Jer. 29:11-13 NIV

9 781944 5665